I Can't Draw A Straight Line With A Ruler

ISSUES IN CREATIVITY AND SPIRITUALITY

Mike Bathum

TRAFFORD

Canada • UK • Ireland • USA • Spain

© Copyright 2004 Mike Bathum.
All rights reserved. No part of this publication may be reproduced, stored in a retrieval system, or transmitted, in any form or by any means, electronic, mechanical, photocopying, recording, or otherwise, without the written prior permission of the author.

Note for Librarians: a cataloguing record for this book that includes Dewey Decimal Classification and US Library of Congress numbers is available from the Library and Archives of Canada. The complete cataloguing record can be obtained from their online database at:
www.collectionscanada.ca/amicus/index-e.html
ISBN 1-4120-4594-0
Printed in Victoria, BC, Canada

TRAFFORD

Offices in Canada, USA, Ireland, UK and Spain
This book was published on-demand in cooperation with Trafford Publishing. On-demand publishing is a unique process and service of making a book available for retail sale to the public taking advantage of on-demand manufacturing and Internet marketing. On-demand publishing includes promotions, retail sales, manufacturing, order fulfilment, accounting and collecting royalties on behalf of the author.
Book sales for North America and international:
Trafford Publishing, 6E–2333 Government St.,
Victoria, BC v8t 4p4 CANADA
phone 250 383 6864 (toll-free 1 888 232 4444)
fax 250 383 6804; email to orders@trafford.com
Book sales in Europe:
Trafford Publishing (uk) Ltd., Enterprise House, Wistaston Road Business Centre,
Wistaston Road, Crewe, Cheshire cw2 7rp United Kingdom
phone 01270 251 396 (local rate 0845 230 9601)
facsimile 01270 254 983; orders.uk@trafford.com
Order online at:
www.trafford.com/robots/04-2402.html

10 9 8 7 6 5 4 3 2

Also by Mike Bathum

The Portfolio of Illustrated 4-Step Art Projects
Simon & Schuster

Discovering Creative Depth Within
The Spirituality of Men: Sixteen Christians Write
About Their Faith
Anthology
Fortress Press

This book is dedicated to those who
follow their creative path

———————————

Acknowledgments

I would like to thank Ben Field and Anna Deeny for their editing skills and enhancing my writing style. To Dorothy Picht for her enthusiasm and feedback while I read portions of each chapter in her presence. To Pat Morrison and Christina Baxter for their wise suggestions in structuring many chapters of this book. And finally to the individuals whose testimonies helped shape this book.

Contents

INTRODUCTION
    I Can't Draw A Straight Line With A Ruler __9

CHAPTER ONE
    The Measure of Our Talent _____17

CHAPTER TWO
    Who's On First _____35

CHAPTER THREE
    Wrapped Up And Mislabeled_____54

CHAPTER FOUR
    Bending and Shaping_____70

CHAPTER FIVE
    Once Upon A Time_____84

CHAPTER SIX
    Skipping Stones _____111

CHAPTER SEVEN
    Looking For Signs_____138

CHAPTER EIGHT
    Sculpting Good Works_____168

POSTSCRIPT_____209

BIBLIOGRAPHY _____215

Introduction

I Can't Draw a Straight Line With a Ruler

Then the Lord rained on Sodom and Gomorrah sulfur and fire from the Lord out of heaven; and he overthrew those cities, and all the Plain, and all the inhabitants of the cities, and what grew on the ground. But Lot's wife, behind him, looked back, and she became a pillar of salt.
Genesis 19: 24-26

Some years ago I was artist-in-residence at a Christian retreat center high in the Cascade Mountains of central Washington State. For a period of seven weeks I taught basic drawing classes to retreatants who had little or no experience in drawing techniques. Most of the adult participants were willing to listen to my techniques on drawing and felt comfortable applying themselves to a creative effort. Some were successful; some were not. We spent most of our time outside in the warm summer sun drawing the surrounding mountains, shapes of trees, and some of the retreat buildings surrounded by varieties of flowers. At the beginning of each class, I guided the students through a specific technique, then let them experience their drawing development on their own before giving one-on-one assistance. I had only one rule: There are no rules, let your drawing flow from your heart, and have fun!

Occasionally I would join the class and draw along with the students. One afternoon we were drawing the interior of one of the large lecture halls. The interior of the room offered a number of interesting subjects. In the center of the hall was a large rock fire pit with split logs placed in the middle. Surrounding the fire pit were fifty to sixty old wooden captain's chairs used during the lecture sessions and for the Sunday worship service. Banners hung from open beam ceilings adding splashes of color to the natural wood walls. A rough fir cross stood at one end of the room. In front of the cross was placed a hewed tree stump fashioned into a pulpit with the inscription, *We Have This Treasure,* carved carefully across the front. It was a beautiful setting but somewhat of a challenge to draw.

After class one afternoon I entered the hall with a large piece of 1/8 inch plywood and a piece of three foot butcher paper taped to the plywood support. I sat in the last row of captain's chairs, placed the plywood backing in my lap with the front edge of plywood supported by the back of the chair directly in front of me, and began to draw. I was drawing with a black ink ball point pen, so any lines I made were permanent. I didn't care if the lines were incorrect; I was trying to capture the spirit of the interior space. The large piece of butcher paper provided the size and range I was looking for.

I was alone in the room when I began the drawing, and as focused as I was on the task at hand, I became aware of a person standing quietly behind me and off to one side. Suddenly I heard a soft woman's voice. "Do you mind if I watch?" she said. "I promise to be quiet, and not disturb you." I turned to see one of my morning students. "Oh, sure," I replied. "I don't mind."

So I began to draw. With sweeping lines I defined the perspective angles of the inside of the hall. Carefully I placed the upright wall structures to the ground plane and sketched the beams across the ceiling to frame the entire room. I drew one of the captain's chairs for size; attaching the legs of the chair to the floor to create the right perspective. The fire pit came next, along with the description of the banners suspended from the beams. I then added the pulpit for size and placed the cross behind, increasing the depth of the interior space.

As I concentrated on my work I was faintly aware of the woman sitting close by.

Sometimes she would stand behind me with her hand resting on the back of my chair so she could have an overview of the development of the drawing. Then she would sit back down again content to stay with me through the duration of the drawing. No one else came into the hall as I added more and more chairs to the drawing, filling in the windows with solid dark areas of ink to give contrast to the line work. Finally I added crosshatching to shade the interior walls and give more complete substance to the chairs, banners, and sanctuary props.

When I was satisfied that I'd completed the drawing, I put my pen down and placed the work against the wall and stood back to observe what I had created. It wasn't a memorable illustration, more an exercise to keep my artistic eye and hand coordination in practice. To this day I can't remember what happened to the drawing, but the conversation I had with the woman after I completed the drawing has remained with me to this day.

She took a chair next to me and gazed at my work. With a sigh she said, "It is so wonderful that you can just sit down and make a complete and beautiful drawing in such a short time." Being a bit humble about praise-on-the-spot I said, "Thank you," and added, "It has always been a creative gift that has come easily to me." After a quiet moment of sharing a view of the drawing she indicated an interest in art. "I've always thought that I would enjoy being an artist but I don't have the talent," she said. I turned toward her. "Well," I began, "much of the work of any artist is desire, skill development, and not being afraid to make mistakes." Suddenly I stepped out of myself as the artist and took the tone of the art teacher. "If you look closely at my drawing you can pick out all kinds of linear mistakes. But I kept working, making corrections as I went and somehow the piece pulled itself together."

The woman didn't seem satisfied with my explanation, becoming defensive in her next statement. "I hear what you're saying but I can't draw a straight line with a ruler!" Not believing what I heard, I became a bit condescending in my tone. "Well of course you can," I heard myself saying, "if you hold the ruler firmly enough with one hand and guide a pencil along the metal strip of the ruler you can execute a perfect line!" She paused for a moment, looked a bit uncomfortable, and continued with her explanation. "But you don't understand, my father told me when I was a child that I shouldn't attempt becoming an artist when I didn't have any skill. He kept telling me I couldn't draw a straight line with a ruler so often that I believe it! It's true... I really can't draw a straight line with a ruler!"

Much time has passed since that mountain retreat conversation but in the passing of time I have heard other adult students express similar statements of restriction that have held a portion of their lives in bondage. To the woman at the retreat center, not drawing a straight line with a ruler was a ruse, a restriction on her freedom placed there by the controlling interests of other voices. To others the words are different, but have the same defeating effect. A successful writer checks his spelling because his older influential brother says he could never spell a word to save his soul. A corporate executive has difficulty making herself clear at meetings because she was called mush-mouth for speaking with her mouth full at the family dinner table when she was a child.

A detail oriented certified public accountant worries endlessly about his client's accounts because he was told by his sixth grade teacher that when he added figures on the blackboard he looked like a chicken-with-his-head-cut-off for being so slow.

The Old Testament story of Lot and his family escaping from God's destruction of Sodom and Gomorrah has a contemporary meaning here. The story presents a paradox for those who have difficulty choosing between what is old and familiar and new and liberating. Lot's wife made the decision to look back at the cities destruction against God's command. In so doing she was turned into a pillar of salt! Rachel Naomi Remen, M.D., describes this action in her book, <u>Kitchen Table Wisdom</u>:

> I suspect that many of us have had this happen to us without our realizing we have become frozen, trapped by the past. We are holding to something long gone and, hands full, are unable to take hold of our opportunities or what life is offering. (p. 195)

The woman watching me draw at the retreat center was trapped by her past, believing the words of her father that she couldn't draw a straight line with a ruler. She was frozen in time and space, as Lot's wife when she looked back at what she left behind.

I have used other voices to describe the influences families and institutions have over us to shape us to their convenience and for their control. It is done when we are children and it is reinforced time and again as we grow into adulthood. And while we strive on our own to make a way in this world we are pulled off course by reminders that we are not good enough. An excellent reminder of this influence is expressed in <u>Your Inner Child of the Past</u>, by W. Hugh Missildine, M.D.

> In our adult lives the "child of the past" is constantly trying to make us live as we lived "at home" in childhood. Due to this influence, we keep twisting our present circumstances and relationships to resemble those we knew in the past. It is not much different in some respects from twisting, curling and rearranging the bedclothes in a certain way as we try to fall asleep in that individual way which each of us has. In this manner we get the "security of the familiar" that we knew as children. While the circumstances and relationships of our early years may not have been entirely comfortable, we learned about life and the world at large in this special childhood setting. We learned to adjust ourselves to this special emotional atmosphere and call it "reality." As adults we tend to continue to see things in terms of the "reality" of this early family setting. (p. 14)

The construction of this book is one attempt to help people recognize the shadowy voices of their past that keeps them from being the full creative and independent people that God intended them to be. The broad overview is written from a Christian perspective and each chapter carries the reader through a set of design prescriptions that are intended to help them mobilize their creative energy, recognize past verbal dysfunction in their lives, guide them through their experiences that have affected the course of their lives , and to work toward creating right thinking and action for possible success based on their own independent thinking.

In discovering words spoken to us from the past, we are caught in a dichotomy of tension: a dynamic between obedience and suffering. We want to be obedient to the past voices of authority that shaped our movements, but suffer because we recognize quite often that words spoken to us in the past create a malaise, restricting us from being our own true selves in the present. Quite often we have no choice but to listen to the verbal abuse when we are young until it cuts a deep, impressionable groove into our memory. Then, when we are adults, we mistreat ourselves and use those same destructive comments passed on to us, short circuiting our own efforts to take risks, find new challenges, or venture into a creative life.

The South Vietnamese Buddhist Monk Thich Nhat Hanh speaks of the Four Noble Truths as a way of recognizing and coming to terms with the idea of suffering. In the Buddhist practice, the First Truth is acknowledging the existence of Suffering. If we do not understand that we are unwell, we cannot find the way to healing. But if we seek help to the First Truth we have an avenue to self-discovery in the Second Truth which is the cause of suffering. The Third Truth follows suit with the possibility of removing the suffering, followed by the Fourth Truth which tells us how to do it.

Each section of the book will have a Christian focused heading followed by a scriptural story that is relevant to the development of the chapter. Personal stories are added that can affect the reader in any number of ways that might bring recognition to their own past histories. Threading through the book are stories of real people who suffered in different categories of life development. We have all been affected in how we were raised in our family of origin, taught to learn a certain way through the educational system, asked or demanded to behave a certain way in a personal relationship, swayed or perhaps bullied to perform in a way that went against our better judgment in our choice of career, or taught to believe in a doctrine of the Church that restricts an individual from thinking independently and making alternate choices that are right for them.

At the end of each chapter is a creative energy assignment designed to help the reader to become focused on a simple design exercise that will involve them in discovering or unlocking their thinking patterns and discovering new and exciting ways at looking at their lives. I call these expressions "ah-ha" experiences designed to help individuals find new directions and break the pattern of what they felt they were incapable of doing, or were held in check by alternate voices in their past. The "prescribed" art projects are simple and easy to perform and are meant to stir up creative energy. They are not meant to make the participants into fine artists, but as unrestricted people who can find ways of problem solving by using simple art techniques.

It can be described as a visual exegesis: art as an avenue toward healing- or- a way of designing a new life!

Chapter One

THE PARABLE OF THE TALENTS

...You ought to have invested my money with the bankers, and my return I would have received what was my own with interest. So take the talent from him, and give it to the one with the ten talents. For to all those who have nothing, even what they have will be taken away. As for this worthless slave, throw him into the outer darkness, where there will be weeping and gnashing of teeth.

Matthew 25: 14-30

Matthew's parable of the talents is an excellent example of putting creative energy to work with a gruesome ending for those who disregard the message. The master of vast property holdings entrusts three servants with his property while he is away on a journey. All three servants are given talents according to their ability. While the master is away the first two servants increase the masters property but the third servant buries the money without regard for increasing the value of the talents that he is responsible for. Upon his return, the master praises the first two servants for increasing his property but is visibly upset with the third servant for burying his money. To make matters worse, the servant called the master a harsh man and that he was afraid of him. Unfortunately for the last servant, the master takes his talents and distributes his share to the other two servants, while the last servant's fate is sealed by being cast into the outer darkness, "where there will be weeping and gnashing of teeth." That's the condensed version of this lengthy parable, but the message is clear.

For the most part this parable is a story about not wasting our talents by neglecting our ability and skill to perform tasks with ease, or to increase the abilities we possess by making good and continual use of them. It makes sense if you think of it in this way: "If you have a talent and don't use it, it becomes rusty and you lose it." But there is more meaning here than just making good use of our giftedness. Biblically, a talent was a measure of money taken from the Greek word *talanton*, meaning weight. In a contemporary, sense talent is a measure of a person's giftedness such as an artist, writer, musician, or an athlete. The New Testament use of the word talent suggests economic power, while the current use of the word indicates personal power. And there is a struggle between the two aspects of power and giftedness going on between the master and the slave. While the master insists upon care for the continuation of his wealth, the servant, although disobedient to the master, seeks personal aptitude on a much different level.

There is the structure of a caste system constructed within Matthew's text where the authority and mastery of a few guide and control the lives and movements of the many. In this case the master is not altogether a good judge of where his servants best talents lie. He seems satisfied that the first two servants are capable of caring for his property and even increasing the value of the property. The third servant doesn't measure up. Although he doesn't increase the value of the property given him, at least he buries it for safe keeping. Does the master not recognize that the last servant may be gifted in other ways? Does he care?

Although the character of the Parable of the Talents is for

us to focus on using our talents, for they are on loan, and to deny them will cause bitter personal disappointment, there is a second message in the text. One of the keys to this parable can be found in the 24th and 25th verse. The servant has an independent mind, telling the master that he is a harsh man, gaining profit for his own purpose without putting in his own effort to work for it. The servant risks everything in speaking out and is in fear for the way the master will punish him verbally. Why is the servant fearful? Has he been dealt with harshly before? The response from the master is quick and harsh..."You wicked and lazy slave," and "As for the worthless slave, throw him into the outer darkness." So although we recognize the obvious message of the Parable of the Talents to use our natural abilities, the stage is also set to recognize that verbal abuse is a common tactic used to deny those who seek their own direction independent of other's need for control.

The servant has spunk and a measure of guts. There is evidence in the parable that he wants to define his own direction, make decisions of how to handle property in his own way. Unfortunately, in biblical times, a servant was considered property of the master and had no rights to make any decisions for choice of life or use of talent. There is more than a hint of defiance and abuse, not too carefully hidden behind the greater lesson of making use of our talents. Here then lies the paradox of a struggle that carries across from biblical times to the present: How does an individual decide to follow his or her own giftedness without the interference of authority? And in what ways can we apply ourselves to new action and direction?

It is not hard to recognize the structures of authoritative controls placed in our path as we grow from children into adulthood, and in some degree or other it comes in stages. The first influence is the family of origin. In this situation the child is asked to be a family game player, to act in accordance with the authority of the parents, to "behave a certain way." Once that is established, the second pressure to conform comes from the educational system where the style of teaching in most cases is streamlined for grouping of students rather than the individual. The call here is to "learn a certain way." Expectations grow in the third stage as a relationship is built between two people. In this case there is a tug-of-war of personalities as each individual tries to determine priorities for each other as to, "be that special person for me in a certain way." In the work place there are clear distinctions between management and labor, superiors and subordinates, supervisor and worker, to meet company expectations. The fourth influence then is for employees on all levels to, "perform in a certain way." Finally, our worship can be influenced by the hierarchical structure of the church so that the faithful are asked, influenced, and even commanded to, "believe in a certain way." In each of these cases the words that are used to influence or coerce people into action can be abusive in nature.

I'VE LOST MY RING

There are many avenues to uncovering creative energy. Consider dream imagery for instance. Frank, a professor of economics at a prestigious university, has spent his tenured career shaping and polishing his students into future businessmen and women ready for the marketplace. His career as a teacher began with the full support of his father who also was a business teacher, before retiring to become a successful small business owner. But Frank has been having a recurring dream suggesting another side of his creative life is trying to get his attention. As Frank begins to describe his dream it becomes apparent that the dream unfolds into an encyclopedia of creative imagery and metaphoric symbolism.

"I am walking into a great hall," Frank begins, " that is barren of any furniture except for a podium at the far end of the room. On the one side of the great hall vertical windows run from floor to ceiling, casting wonderful light onto the polished hardwood floor and the soft white walls. There is a man sitting on a high chair next to the podium dressed in soft linen garments. He is writing on a piece of paper but stops and focuses on my approach. He asks me how he might be of service to me. I hold up my right hand and tell him I have lost my college class ring. He asks me to describe what it looks like. I'd worn the ring so long that I stopped looking at it and couldn't remember what it looked like. The man encouraged me to close my eyes and focus on the ring in my mind and think of symbols that gave the ring shape and definition. After some thought I began to describe the color and shape of the ring, the class year and university name, school motto and crest. As I spoke the man was making line drawings of strange structural shapes on the paper. When I'd finished speaking the man handed the paper to me and asked me to leave the room and search for the ring out in the country. I thought the drawings on the paper were to be a map as a guide to find the ring. But as I left the room I stepped outside into a great city and got on a bus that was waiting for me. I sat behind the bus driver who was a woman dressed in a green uniform. There was a man sitting near the rear of the bus whose features were dark and undistinguishable who was wearing a black sweater and pants. He gave me side glances occasionally, but spent most of his attention gazing out the bus window. He made no attempt to talk with me. As we drove through the city, many tall skyscrapers were still under construction and looked like some of the sketches the man made on the paper. Finally the dream ended as we drove into the countryside where scenery of unmatched beauty opened up before us revealing green fields, clusters of trees and small well-tended farms. The bus driver opened the door to let me out and remarked that I be aware of the beauty before me and to begin my search for my class ring."

Concerned about the repeated pattern of the dreams, Frank sought the assistance of a psychotherapist to help him begin to untangle the unconscious nighttime imagery and bring it into reality. Over a period of a few months, the therapist helped Frank shed light on the meaning of the dream. Before Frank became an economics professor, he was interested in pursuing a degree in fine art. As a young high school student he was always drawing rough thumbnail sketches of buildings and took several drawing and design classes to sharpen his technical abilities and learn the importance of perspective, design principals, and color ranges.

But as Frank moved toward a college choice in painting and drawing, his father intervened between Frank and his love of visual art, imposing his strong will to effectively change Frank's mind from pursuing art to following business. Joe always said "art is a useless pursuit and not a responsible way to earn a living." The word "responsible" left a strong impact on Frank. So strong, in fact, that he gradually left his talent for drawing behind in favor of degree work in economics and business administration that would make him responsible in the eyes of his father.

Further analysis with the therapist revealed the symbols of the dream. Frank's ring represented a powerful sign of the continuous cycle of life. In his case it was his missing college ring that indicated that he had lost his way and his purpose of attending college to study art. The large empty room represented the emptiness of the inner being that only came through in his unconscious state. But searching for the ring indicated that he wanted to reconnect with his primary giftedness. The man at the podium drawing lines on paper, representing a portion of his own inner personality, made reference to Frank's inner energy and drive using the drawing on the paper as a map to help him find his way.

Frank seemed to recognize the implication of boarding the bus and sitting close to the female driver in the green uniform without much coaxing from the therapist. He thought the bus represented the way he got around in life and the woman in the green uniform was indicative of the desire to nurture one's self into new growth. Frank wrestled with the image of the dark male figure sitting in the back of the bus. With the therapist's help, Frank recognized an interesting dichotomy taking place. He could see the dark figure representing the dark side of his personality, but at the same time the shadowy figure was his father keeping an eye on him. Interestingly, Frank indicated that he alone got off the bus and the dark man remained behind, and eventually disappeared from sight as the bus drove away.

The dream sequences began shortly after Frank's father passed away. Although Frank always felt that he was trapped by the words of the past, carrying around a taped message in his head the words and wishes of his father who weighed in favor of responsible living versus the uselessness of art as a way of living. Frank's unconscious information was reconnecting him to his creative side in the dream sequences. Now he had the opportunity to change the tapes of the past for his own taping session and join the separate sides of himself: the linear, practical work of his business practices with the emotional, holistic work of the creative artist. Frank expressed to the therapist that it felt like someone had opened the window to his world and fresh air was coming into the room and he was taking his first deep breath in years.

Each person is affected in some way in their lives by the way people talk about them.

Class distinction, wealth or fame does not exempt us from the harsh reality of being verbally maligned. Throughout Joe Dimaggio's life and baseball career he suffered from shyness and self doubt that is well documented in Richard Ben Cramer's book, <u>Joe Dimaggio, The Hero's Life.</u>

> Joe's second school, two blocks east, was Francisco Junior High. Nobody made him do anything there. Joe and Frank Venezia used to sit in class like a couple of dummies-they never kept up on the reading. The other kids gave all the answers. They just seemed smarter. Actually, Joe wasn't stupid. But he never wanted to open his mouth, say something wrong, and *look* stupid. That came from home. In the flat on Taylor Street, they talked Sicilian. Everybody laughed at Joe's lousy Sicilian. (Even his little brother, Dommie, made fun of him.) And shame was what Joe couldn't stand. He was a blusher. (That embarrassed him, too.) So, he

just grew silent. His sisters talked about him behind his back: they thought he was "slow." ...Anyway, Joe didn't have to talk at school. None of the teachers made him talk. They just moved him on, year after year. It was like no one ever knew he was there. (p. 7)

SIMPLE INNOVATION

When I was a young graduate student in fine arts I was half way through my masters degree program trying to shape a thesis statement and find a creative direction for my painting. There were several other painting candidates in my class who were struggling with the same issues, hoping that some bright light would illuminate their stretched canvases and guide their brush strokes into a new world of artistic acceptance, anything that would please our painting professor who held our degree hopes like a carrot before us. Would we make it, or would we not?

During the winter quarter of the second and final year of studies, the class left the painting annex at the university after a lengthy Saturday studio workshop. We had just finished a grueling critique of our work by the fine arts faculty and were heading for our cars in the nearby parking lot, thankful that we had escaped the critical exposure of our paintings with our lives still intact. We were not in the best of spirits, and wondered if painting was the artistic direction we should be pursuing. Our heads were full of doubts of why our creative efforts were stuck in place!

The weather that winter term was especially cold and snowy. The parking lot had been cleared of snow the previous day but ice had formed, making driving a clear hazard. One of our group was an especially gifted painter, a woman who seemed secure in her development right from the beginning of the first year of her studies. But as the second year moved along and the critiques of her work became more critical and harsh, she began to worry about her skill as an artist. As she described her feelings as a painter, it was her dark night of the soul.

As we all prepared to leave, we gathered around her car as she sat somewhat dejected behind the wheel with the motor running. We tried to cheer her up but she wasn't accepting our commiserations. She put the car in gear and tried to move forward but the car didn't move. The tires were spinning, making that high pitched whine tires make when they can't get traction on ice. We all gave her our best snow driving advise. "Don't give it too much gas," we said. "Try putting it in reverse, then put it in forward to break the grip of the ice on the tires," we suggested. Nothing happened, the car didn't move. Puzzled, we finally gave up and all of us gathered at the rear of her car and began to push. Nothing doing, the car still didn't move! Finally I walked up to the driver's side of the car and peered in. Something clicked in my mind. "Release the hand brake," I said. The woman released the hand brake and the car moved out of the parking lot without delay. "Ah-ha," she said as she waved with new found pleasure and sped away. "Ah-ha," we said, as we returned her wave and looked at one another in surprise and amazement.

Something was released in all of us that winter day. We thought we had the right answer to free the car from its icy grip. It was the unexpected, the logical resolution of the problem that corrected our thinking. It was the same for us in finding new direction for our painting. Releasing the car's brake was the metaphoric catalyst that shaped us to think in a new creative way. We needed to let go of our expectations and limitations of what we thought our work should look like so that we could discover new and exciting "Ah-ha" experiences and find new dimensions to our creative energy.

Project: Graph Design

The first design project is a simple way to release the energy found in all of us. The design is like the shape and body of a car. It is self contained and easy to set into motion, especially if the participant releases the hand brake (in this case "lets go of their expectations and limitations"). Although the design project in question is small in size it has the capacity for enlargement depending upon the adventurous nature of the designer. Since this is the first assigned creative release, there are materials to gather and some guidelines to follow. Illustrations will follow to guide the participant visually in the preparation for play. I am leaving the word "work" out of the dialogue, allowing the generative energy of those who participate to flow freely.

The materials needed are simple. A piece of graph paper, a number 2 soft leaded pencil, eraser, and assorted color pencils are all that are required. The graph paper will have light blue lines running both vertically and horizontally through the whole page. It is preferable that the intersecting lines on the page contain five squares per square inch. If the line structure is too tight, such as eight or ten squares per inch, the lines that form the squares will be too small to create a meaningful design.

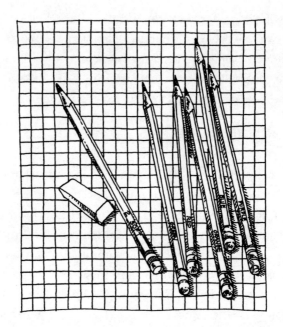

The guidelines to this project act as the rules-of-the-road and the illustrations are the visual signposts that help the creative project come to an understandable conclusion.

To begin the undertaking, find one square inch unit-of-squares anywhere on the graph paper. Keep in mind one square inch unit will isolate 25 small squares that constitute the shape the design is called for. Exactly in the center of that square unit there is a square equally distant from the top, bottom, and both sides of the square. That square will act as the central focal point to the design. The second guideline calls for the development of a symmetrical design on all four sides of the central square. That means an individual will be creating a design that repeats exactly the same to the left and right vertically and horizontally of the central square. The number 2 pencil is used to form the line structure in each square and the eraser is used occasionally to make changes if needed. The following illustrations demonstrate this activity.

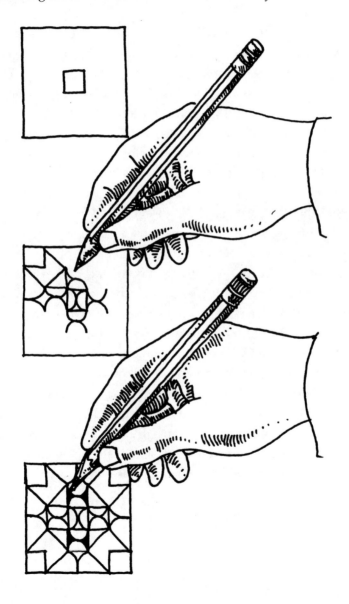

The graph lines that surround and run through the design are a comfort to the initiate, offering a controlled template and a point of reference in which to play with tangible concepts in the form of drawn lines and shapes. The freedom to express different line shapes can be seen as time goes on: diagonal lines running from corner to corner, circles or half circles filling different squares, small squares within large squares, gentle curved lines throughout, and so forth.

Once the participant has successfully completed a design that meets with their satisfaction, color patterns may be considered. The third guideline then is to fill in the design shapes with colors. For best results some squares can be filled in with color while other areas of the design could be left as white areas to create contrast and interest. Color choices should be made carefully. If two dark colors, such as purple and blue, are placed next to each other, some of the design pattern will look like one shape instead of two, thereby weakening the overall design. Try and remember to place a dark color next to a light color for a strong visual impact and a more interesting design. Good contrast choices would include black against white, blue next to orange, green against red, purple across from yellow. All of these contrasting colors are the basic building blocks on a standard color wheel. Keep in mind the color patterns will repeat the same in each drawn pattern that forms the overall symmetrical design of the one inch square unit. The following example demonstrates this clearly.

To this point the pattern that is created is a design on purpose. The participant has created a design out of his or her own consciousness. Concepts have been liberated from the mind and arranged on the graph paper and reinterpreted as tangibles. It's the beginning of a new creation. What happens in the next guideline begins to change the rules of the designing road so that what a person creates will bring forth something not foreseen, or a new creation that happens by accident.

The fourth guideline states that a second graph design be created exactly like the first one and placed directly to the left or right side of the first design on the graph paper. Draw all the lines and place all the same colors in the squares so that the second image looks exactly like the first one. Once the two designs are complete, notice the new design shape that has taken place between the two designs as they touch each other. This is a design that happens by accident, or if you like, the beginning of the "ah-ha" experience! The following illustration lets the viewer see the second creative shapes.

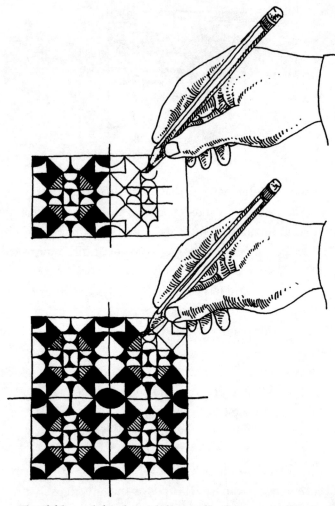

The fifth and final guideline asks the experimenting participant to create two additional square unit designs exactly as the first two appear. These two additional units are to be placed just above or below the first two designs, making a big block of four designs involving 100 individual squares. At the center of this new block of squares, an additional design shape appears that, again, happens by accident. Now the design has expanded, giving the project a range of possibilities to experiment with, that were not possible before. Instead of one design that was labored over, a new set of patterns have emerged. One design has increased to two, and again to three, and finally four, with elements of other shapes spinning off to create other shapes as the eye follows across the entire piece of craftsmanship.

In the midst of the project, clear cut objectives were forming along with the conscious effort to develop a pleasing design. Those objectives could be stated first as a way to develop simple design elements within a very limited space. Second, to make a unique visual statement. Third, to construct imaginative patterns of dark and light. Fourth, to create visual rhythm through color patterns and shapes, and finally, to take risks and explore new ways of thinking and processing with conceptional themes. There were controls involved with the basic concept of the project in the beginning, to keep the uninitiated designer from being intimidated. However, as the design developed, new freedom of expression was realized and a refreshing release of energy could be felt as an "ah-ha" experience.

Shaun McNiff, in his book, <u>Art as Medicine,</u> explains the outcome of creative expression, whether it be a simple design, a doodle, or a expansive painting:

> The painting I make can change my life. Rather than revealing something about who I was when they were created, the images will sometimes make a statement influencing what I will become. As the images change, I change. I can never be sure which is having the

primary influence on the other. Creation is a collaborative process and an intimate relationship between artists and their materials in which the participants continually transform one another. (p. 64)

Chapter Two

A Man Born Blind Receives Sight

Jesus said, "I came into this world for judgment so that those who do not see may see, and those who do see may become blind."

John 9: 39

The ninth chapter of the Gospel of John is devoted to Jesus giving the gift of sight to a man born blind. It is a long chapter to devote to one healing and there are many characters in this performance to keep track of, so the reader needs to pay close attention. The cast include Jesus, His disciples, the man born blind from birth, the blind man's neighbors, the Pharisees, and the blind man's parents. While there is an inspirational and serious message running through the ninth chapter, one can't help but note a thread of humor present in the entire story.

The plot, in a way, is reminiscent of Abbott and Costello's classic comedy skit, *Who's On First?* The same kind of misunderstandings exist in both the blind man's healing in the Gospel of John and Abbott and Costello's stand-up routine: the cast of characters can't believe what they are hearing. In the skit taken from the early 1950's television show, *The Colgate Comedy Hour,* Bud Abbott has been named the manager of the Colgate Baseball Team. Lou Costello is pleased with Bud's achievement and asks for the names of the players and the positions they play. The comedy routine begins in this manner of confusion.

Abbott: "Let's see... on the team Whos on first, Whats on second, and I Don't Know on third."

Costello: "Are you the manager?"

Abbott: "Yes! "

Costello: "Do you know the guys names?"

Abbott: "I should. "

Costello: "You wanna tell me the guys names?"

Abbott: "I say Whos on first, Whats on second, I Don't Know on third."

Costello: "Are you the manager?"

Abbott: "Yes!"

Costello: "You know the guys names?"

Abbott: "I'm telling you their names!"

Costello: "Well, who's on first?"

Abbott: "Yes!"

Costello: "Well, go ahead and tell me!"

Abbott: "Who!"

Costello: "The – guy – on – first!"

Abbott: "WHO!"

Costello: "The – guy – playing – first – base!"

Abbott: "WHO!"

Costello: "The guy on first!"

Abbott: "Who is on first!"

Costello: "WHAT ARE YOU ASKING ME FOR,...I'M ASKING YOU!"

Abbott: "I"M NOT ASKING YOU, ... I'M TELLING YOU!"

Costello: "You ain't telling me nothing! I'm asking you who's on first?"

Abbott: "That's it!"
Costello: "Well go ahead and tell me!"
Abbott: "Who!"
Costello: "The – GUY – on – first – base!"
Abbott: "That's his name."
Costello: "That's whose name?"
Abbott: "YES!"
Costello: "Well go ahead and tell me!"
Abbott: "That's the man's name!"
Costello: "That's whose name?
Abbott: "YES!"
Costello: "Well, go ahead and tell me!"
Abbott: "Who is on first!"
Costello: "WHAT ARE..YOU…ASKING…ME…FOR!! I'M ASKING…YOU…WHO'S…ON…FIRST!"
Abbott: "That's it!!"
Costello: "Well go ahead and tell me!"
Abbott: "Who!"
Costello: "THE GUY ON FIRST!!"
Abbott: "That's it!"
Costello: "What's the guy's name on first?"
Abbott: "No, Whats on second! "

What makes this a classic bit of comedy is in the way the routine is set up. Abbott knows the players names, and so does the audience. However, Costello plays the fall guy who is not able to interpret simple words usually associated as verbs in sentence structure and reinterpreted as the subject in the sentence as nouns.

In the Gospel of John, Jesus uses a similar tactic in the 9th Chapter to perform a miracle. He makes the blind man see to confound the Pharisees who adhere strictly to the law of keeping the Sabbath holy. The whole issue is stated clearly in verse 16. Some of the Pharisees said, "This man is not from God, for he does not observe the sabbath." So in this narrative, Jesus knows all the cast of characters, the blind man knows that he can see, the disciples, neighbors, and the blind man's parents all stand apart, generally participating, but mostly witnessing the development of the scene taking place.

That leaves the Pharisees in confusion, as the action unfolds in the healing story. Here now is a similar script in a Biblical form of *Who's On First* as the Pharisees can't believe what they are hearing.

Pharisees: "How did you receive your sight?"
Man: "He put mud on my eyes. Then I washed, and now I see."
Others: "How can a man who is a sinner perform such signs?"
Pharisees: "What do you say about him?"
Man: "He is a prophet."
Pharisee: (To the parents) "Is this your son, who you say was born blind?"
Parents: "We know this is our son, but we do not know how it is that he is able to see. Ask him, he is of age."
Pharisees: "But this man is a sinner!"
Man: "One thing I do know, I was blind, but now I see."
Pharisees: "How did he open your eyes?"
Man: "I've told you already! Why do you want to hear it again?"
Pharisees: "You are his disciple!"
Man: "If this man were not from God, he could do nothing."

Pharisee: "You were born in sin, and your trying to teach
    us?"
Jesus: "I came into this world so that those who do not see
    may see, and those who do see may become blind."
Pharisees: "Surely we are not blind, are we?"

So Jesus turns the tables on the Pharisees by countering their strict adherence to following the sabbath rule by entering his own countermand. "I came into this world for judgment so that those who do not see may see, and those who do see may become blind." (John 9: 39) The Pharisees are so confused at this point, that they question themselves before the whole audience. "Surely we are not blind, are we? "(John 9: 40) They have not only guessed the answer to their own question, but have attempted to cover their own defeat by denouncing the man who had been blind. Just as Lou Costello could not accept the players names, the Pharisees could not see the creative way Jesus brings new life to the blind man.

Not being able to see constitutes all kinds of problems. Suppose all those present in the story of the blind man were all members of the same family. In this case the family is based upon the classic hierarchical structure known as the ladder formula: power comes from the top down. The Pharisees would represent the authority, setting guidelines for the rest of the family to follow. The rest of the family members play their roles in character to the authority figure. The blind man's parents acquiesce to the authority of the Pharisees because they are afraid that they could be driven out of the synagogue. The blind man assumes his position in the family order as long as he remains blind. The neighbors and other bystanders play their minor part of the family as well, not only accepting their positions, but agreeing with the family standards the Pharisees have set forth. They brought to the Pharisees the man who had formerly been blind, (John 9: 13) saying, "How can a man who is a sinner perform such signs?" (John 9: 16)

Sometimes in families, the authority figure doesn't always represent the best interest of the other family members. A repressive arrogation of authority can easily suppress individual freedoms and creativity. However, as long as all the members play their part in the family, at least on the surface, the system seems to work. But if someone steps out of character, the balance of power is threatened and the individual relationships take on a much different manner.

When Jesus enters into the scene of the blind man, He describes in verse 3 that the man was born blind so that God's work might be revealed in him. But Jesus healing the blind man is only the beginning of some remarkable transformations taking place in the name of God. While we see the tangible evidence of healing being performed, Jesus is also changing the structure of authority by breaking the Sabbath rule. The hierarchical framework under the watchful eye of the Pharisees is being converted to a linear apportionment, giving freedom to individuals within the system to have options: to see, hear, and act differently on their own merits. As the framework changes, so does the attitude of the Pharisees. They are threatened, confused, and act consistently throughout the Gospels to find ways to silence Jesus for His teachings and healing ministry (Matt 26: 3, Mk 14: 1, Lk 22:1 and Jn 11: 47).

Although Jesus makes a quick transition from healing the blind man in Chapter 9 to the story of the good shepherd in Chapter 10, there is a lingering desire to stay with the man with new sight both literally and figuratively. Now that he can see his surroundings, how does he look upon the members of his family? Certainly he doesn't need support to get from one place to another. He may find work or some creative outlet with his new ability to see. The man may even decide to leave the family and seek life on his own. Regardless, his transformation has created a dichotomy of vision. How do his parents react to his new vision and independence? We do not know. Much like the Pharisees however, they may feel threatened and find their authority diminished. In this case to see is liberating, and not to see is confining.

Getting in Each Others Way

When I was a young child, I remember a special room my father kept locked up in the corner of our upstairs bedroom. We lived in a large two story house and the bedroom was unused except for the occasional activity carried on by my father in that special room. I thought it was all very mysterious until he invited me into the room one day to witness a fascinating creative process evolving in the dark. He had enlarged the closet in the bedroom to accommodate a photography darkroom. The room was filled with trays of pungent smelling liquids. There were clotheslines strung across the room with photos hanging like my mother's laundry put out to dry in the basement. There was an enlarger, boxes of photographic paper, rolls of film, a small refrigerator, several cameras, unusual gadgets, and strips of negatives sharing the clothesline with the drying photos. The room was painted black and a heavy dark curtain hung suspended across the doorway. The whole room was made even more mysterious when he started to work, turning out the bright overhead light to work by the dim glow of a single red bulb.

Being admitted into my father's private world of photography was my first evidence of his passion for creative self expression. Unfortunately, photography was not his business, but his hobby. He was, by career, a certified public accountant for a large international construction company. Much of his work kept him away from home, following construction crews to exotic places around the world, tracking money earned, and money spent. But when he was home, photographic activity continued upstairs in the enlarged closet.

More and more I spent time with my dad in that special room as he taught me some of the fundamentals of photography. As he explained how to load film into a camera, or instructed me on how to develop film, he used a curious statement to emphasize a point. He would look at me and say, "Se Stue? "I never knew the exact meaning of the words, or whether it was just a strange mannerism he used, but I always understood it to mean, do you see? "Yes," I would say, "I see."

In contrast, my mother was a college graduate with a degree in journalism. When she met and eventually married my father, she put aside her professional writing skills to become a homemaker and look after my two brothers and myself. She had a passion for environmental issues and often wrote letters to newspapers and articles for nature newsletters supporting wildness and conservation. We called her the gray-haired environmentalist and she took pride in the skillful articles she wrote to inform the community of the dangers affecting our surroundings.

When I was still in elementary school, my father and

mother agreed it was time to break away from the city, the large two story house, and the corporate job to seek a simpler life style in the country as dairy farmers. As we closed the upstairs darkroom, carefully packing all the photographic equipment in boxes, my father confided in me that a darkroom would be built in our new house, one that would accommodate a professional direction and not just a passive hobby. With renewed vigor, and a smile he would look at me and say, "Se Stue?" "Yes," I would respond, "I see."

But dairy farming was not a good choice. Keeping cows in production, buying equipment and erecting new buildings to make a profit kept my father tied to the construction firm to pay for the farm upkeep and expansion. While my dad was away on business trips, my mother took charge of the farm. My brothers and I did what we could to help make the dairy run efficiently but it was clear, that for our family, farming was a losing proposition. Soon the balance of authority began to spin out of control. As my brothers and I grew into our teenage years we began to develop other interests. My older brother chose scouting, my younger brother busied himself with sports, which left me in the middle supporting my mother on the dairy, choosing 4H and finding artistic outlets in school.

Tension finally erupted one summer day as the three of us were shooting baskets into the hoop erected on the garage wall next to the house. Soon we could hear, over the bouncing basketball and the squeaking of our tennis shoes against the cement driveway, the raised voices of our parents arguing in the house. We stopped playing and stared in the living room window amazed at my mother and father squaring off at each other. Alarmed, I put the basketball down and headed for the back door to find out what was going on. But my mother intercepted me before I could step inside the house. With tears in her eyes, and a tissue in her hand, she asked us to remain outside until they had resolved their discussion.

Hours later, my mother came to the door with a smile on her face, announcing that it was ok for us to come into the house. As we entered the living room my father was sitting on the couch with his head bent low, his eyes fixed on his hands folded carefully in his lap. There was a sadness in his appearance that I had not witnessed before. My mother, on the other hand, looked relieved and refreshed. However placid the atmosphere seemed at the moment, there was not an explanation forthcoming from either my father or my mother about the heated discussion that lasted the better part of a day.

Weeks afterward, my mother, who had a new degree of assurance, divulged what had taken place during that long argument in the living room. Apparently my father had had enough of working as a business accountant. He wanted to sell the farm and invest his talent and energy in professional photography while he still had some working years left to him. My mother was vehemently opposed to the idea, argued throughout the day that quitting his lucrative business position would jeopardize their financial future and destroy the continuation of the farm. Little by little my father gave ground to her arguments, but held on to the hope that his dream of becoming a photographer could be realized. Finally by late afternoon a compromise was reached. My mother agreed with my dad to sell the dairy, and she, in turn, would cancel any aspirations she had to become a working journalist. She would devote all her time to holding the marriage and family together. In the bargain my father lost the vision that he prized most; becoming a photographer. To keep the peace in the family he gave up his dream and would continue working as a certified public accountant.

From that day forward, in little degrees, my father's appearance and energy level began to change. He became distant, and the sparkle seemed to fade in his eyes. When my parents eventually sold the farm and moved to a house in town, he retreated to the privacy of their new TV room where he watched golf matches and ate chocolate ice cream. His behavior became reclusive, and his movements, sedentary. There was no mention of a new darkroom, and the stored photographic equipment remained in their boxes. My father lost interest in giving me more lessons, and we never again exchanged the words that meant so much between us…"Se Stue?" "Yes, I see."

But in the error of such a pivotal family argument the empowerment of creative life held by my parents was canceled, washed away in one day and exchanged for the sake of safety and security. Keeping the status quo within the existing family structure was their form of keeping a holy encumbrance. My father relinquished his creative desire to become a photographer and my mother lost the chance to use her power with words. Bitterness resulted between them. In a strange way, denying their creativity was like each of them taking a toxic pill; each took the poison, hoping the other would die! My father once had a vision, a dream, seeing it in his mind, and touching it with his hands, only to have it slip away so easily. Once he could see, but then he became blind.

Both my parents have passed away and it wasn't until recently that I could pick up the theme of sight that was present in their lives. I began to wonder, how could I honor their unused creative life through my own? I've been a productive artist all my life, matching, in a way, with paint and pencil, the photographic talent of my father. I'm also an author, sharing the skills my mother displayed so often in her early life. When I was young I was too low on the family hierarchy structure to help my parents resolve their issues. But now I have the chance to effectively honor the creative energy that belonged to them and can be used through me!

The Buddhist tradition has a wonderful way of honoring and celebrating parents and all ancestry through a practice called the recitations of the Five Awarenesses. The recitation is taken from the <u>Chanting and Recitation Book,</u> compiled by Thich Nhat Hanh. After each verse is read, a bell is rung so that those who hear what is being read may reflect and meditate on each awareness and note how it affects their lives. The verses have particular meaning in this last story:

> We are aware that all generations of our ancestors
> and all future generations are present in us.
> (Bell)
> We are aware of the expectations that our ancestors,
> our children, and their children, and their children
> have of us.
> (Bell)
> We are aware that our joy, peace, freedom, and harmony are the joy, peace, freedom, and harmony
> of our ancestors, our children, and their children.
> (Bell)
> We are aware that understanding is the very foundation of love.
> (Bell)

> We are aware that blaming and arguing can never help us
> and only create a wider gap between us;
> that only understanding, trust, and love
> can help us change and grow.
> (Two Bell) (p. 35, 36)

By being cognizant that my parents were an influential part of my life, I am able to reflect on how much they suffered by their refusal to participate in their own creative energy. They suffered, and I suffer for them. Despite the choices they made I cannot deny my creative side; it nags at me if I do! So as I paint I borrow some of the creative energy of my father's talent, and honor him as I do so. And when I write I have some of my mother's gift at my fingertips, and I honor her creativity as well.

Project: A Circle and Line Design

The second design project takes into account a portion of Jesus' statement…" so that those who do not see may see…" found in the 9th chapter of the Gospel of John. The ingredients to this piece are elements that we recognize in everyday life, but when applied to a design concept it is hard to understand, or see, what the outcome will be. The elements involved is a circle and four lines. Many readers might think that much design work can't take place with such a limited number of elements to work with. So some investigative work must take place before the project begins.

Once again the materials needed are simple. A piece of white paper, a pencil, ruler, small jar lid or coin, and an assortment of colored pencils or colored ink pens will be all that the participant needs. In the beginning the size of the design is not important. Since the design requirements are specific and limited, thumbnail sketches may help the individual until a desired design is achieved.

To get started, the designing participant will draw a round circle at the top of the paper using the small jar lid or a quarter as a template. Next to the circle draw four straight lines of equal length using the ruler as a guide. This gives the designer a reference to go by. The idea of the design project is to connect all four lines at their ends in a crossing pattern and overlapping the circle. The next illustration demonstrates my point.

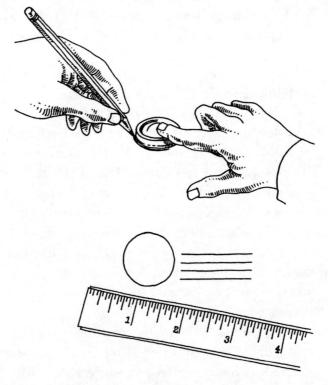

The ability to make a creative design using such restrictive elements is quite limited in scope. So the next part of the project requires the participant to ask some probing questions before they get down to describing their project. For instance, does the circle have to be perfectly round? No, the only requirement is that the line forming the circle must be completely closed. It may also be larger in size than the outline created by the template. The next obvious question concerns the size of the lines. Does each line have to be the same length? Not only can the lines be of different lengths, but they can bend and some can be thicker, while other lines are thinner. Finally, do the intersecting lines need to be contained within the inside of the circle? No, some of the lines may break the plane of the circle, while others are contained inside the sphere. Or, all intersecting lines may connect with each other outside the circle. While the ingredients in the design phase have now changed for more creative flexibility, the basis rules of the project still apply: the four lines must touch each other at the ends and intersect inside and through the circle.

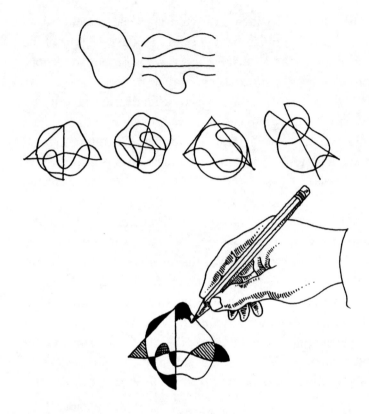

At the beginning of this project it is a good idea to develop a number of basic designs without thinking what the outcome may be. This is a time to be playful, leaving your reasoning powers by the wayside and not thinking about the result of your creations. The best way to describe this concept is through M.C. Richards statement, in her book, <u>Centering: In Pottery, Poetry, and the Person</u>. There is a ..."need for spontaneous human feeling." She follows that remark by indicating that, "Working with our materials as artist-craftsmen may help to engender a new health here." (pg. 17, 18)

It is hard to keep the results of what the designer creates

once several thumbnails have been completed. With just four lines arranged playfully and thoughtfully through a misshaped circle, some interesting shapes begin to take form. So as the creative person observes the designs and begins to feel an "ah-ha" experience taking shape, consider that one of the primary outcomes of this assignment is to, quite literally, see shapes that have a defined meaning and recognition. For instance, do you see a number shape, or a letter form? Is there the shape of an animal, human, or a manufactured object in your design? These visions may, or may not, appear as part of your design. Failure (a word we should not include in our vocabulary) to see recognizable objects in the designs should not be a limiting factor in this assignment. Abstract images are evidence of creativity just as much as the development of formal recognizable shapes. One thing is sure: You are giving freedom to your creative process by massaging your brain!

The second outcome of this assigned project, whether the participant realizes it or not, is to make use of the elements and principles of art. Line, space, color, texture, shape, form, balance, contrast, focal point, rhythm, and unity come into play. A short explanation of each design principle would be of use here. The most obvious element in this assigned project is line. Line is a path created by a moving point. Using line can show direction, divide a space and represent an object. Next, space is created by the very act of a moving point of lines interconnecting with each other.

Space can be characterized in two ways. It can be a positive indicating a foreground area which draws a viewers attention first. Or space can be a negative, in which case the background predominates in strength over the foreground. Color is a strong factor in any design and will lend a strong impact in this project. Texture implies a tactile surface related to touch in a three-dimensional sense, or implied and visual that can be seen but not felt, in a two-dimensional design. Though texture is a strong element of art, its usage here will not be discussed. The element of shape will be evident in this assigned piece as it will take most of the creative effort to find those recognizable or abstract shapes.

The principles of art are represented first by balance. Balance can be seen in three ways. First, the design can be informal or asymmetrical indicating unequal parts. Since this work is freeform, the primary design will take an informal look initially. Second, balance can be achieved by a formal or symmetrical appearance where equal distribution of identical parts appear on both sides of a central axis. Finally, radical balance has a central point which the design radiates from and around. Contrast is the second principal. Contrast suggests opposition or variety in a design such as light and dark, or rough and smooth. Using contrast can add a richness to the project. The use of dark and light colors in the participant's work will give this impression. Third, a focal point creates a center of emphasis or interest that will draw the eye into the design.

The last two principles are rhythm and unity. Rhythm is the quality of visual movement. It can be created by repeating similar elements throughout the project. The rhythm of line will be most evident in the creation of the circle and line design. Finally, unity is the quality of a unified whole. All parts unite to give a feeling of a total relationship in the structure of the design being developed. All of the elements and principles of art can be applied to all the art projects assigned in this book, so referring to them now and again will be helpful throughout each piece of assigned work.

The strong use of the element of color will help bring this assigned project closure. As I indicated in the graph design, the participant should keep the color patterns in a contrasting range so that each individual shape within the design stands out. Black against white, green next to red, blue side by side with orange, and so on. With the number of thumbnail sketches arranged on the paper, contrasting colors can be played with until the right color pattern is arrived at by the initiate. Each person has a different approach to design and color pattern arrangement, so individual development, or what I call a "critical eye," becomes the "ah-ha" experience in this assignment. "Yes," you can say to yourself with satisfaction, "I do see!"

Chapter Three

RAISING LAZARUS FROM THE DEAD

...he cried out with a loud voice, "Lazarus, come out!" The dead man came out, his hands and feet bound with strips of cloth, and his face wrapped in a cloth. Jesus said to them "Unbind him, and let him go."

John 11: 43-44

"Sticks and stones may break my bones, but names will never hurt me!" We're all familiar with this age old youthful verse. It's the simplest defensive tactic to guard ourselves from being hurt by those who attack us verbally. I first heard the term in elementary school when a group of children were taunting another student. Even though the saying has a nice ring to it, and is used as a counter measure to protect the self from being hurt, it very rarely works. Somehow the belittling words always find a chink in the armor of another and the damage is done.

Are you familiar with the saying, "You couldn't hit the broad side of a barn if your life depended on it." or "What a klutz you are!" Mild rejoinders meant to poke harmless fun, right? How about something a little more mean spirited. Have comments like, "Stupid is as stupid does," "Ugly as a mud fence," or, "Hey, four eyes," been aimed your way? At one time or another we have all had to endure the adverse affects of name calling, so we know the pain it can cause.

More recently, belittling words and taunting practices

have taken a horrible direction. Those individuals who have endured the name calling of others settle the score with the use of a handgun, carrying out their rage indiscriminately, inflicting injury and death upon their peers, whether they were part of the taunting or not. The lives of all involved are forever altered. It vividly points out what Rachel Naomi Remen, M.D. states in her book, <u>Kitchen Table Wisdom</u> that.."The life in us is diminished by judgment far more frequently than by disease." Verbal acts of judgment can bind us in despair, entombing our lives and rigidly wrapping ourselves useless to a productive future and a creative life. It certainly brings to light what Lazarus had to endure.

Imagine the difficulty Lazarus had in the illness and death story found in the Eleventh chapter of John. Mary and Martha had pronounced to Jesus that their brother had been ill and now was dead, laying wrapped in a burial cloth and entombed for four days. Jesus didn't seem too concerned about the plight of Lazarus as he waited two days "where he was" before attending to Lazarus near Bethany after receiving the news that he was dead. But the delay created the kind of drama that would bring Jesus glory and Lazarus back from the deep sleep of death.

Once the rock was removed from the tomb and Lazarus emerged wrapped head to toe in strips of cloth, the sight must have created surprise and shock from those who thought him dead. A person tightly wrapped in a burial cloth would present a ghostly apparition, creating the kind of mood that made Boris Karloff movies so scary. With a body cast of tightly wrapped cloth Lazarus, it would be imagined, could hardly walk with his arms pinned and immobilized at his side. His head certainly would have been fixed without the ability to turn in either direction and Lazarus would have had extreme difficulty seeing through the cloth covering his head. Sitting in such a situation would be out of the question, but losing one's balance and falling was a distinct possibility.

The revolutionary power of Jesus' words to Lazarus is what gives this Gospel story strength. Most of Jesus' ministry was devoted to providing healing for people that affected a part of their lives: healing a leper (Matthew 8), casting out a demon (Mark 7), healing a handicapped woman (Luke 13). But with Lazarus, Jesus brings back from death the whole body, mind and spirit of his friend. Imagine being restored fully with the command, "Lazarus, come out!" And Lazarus came bound up in the grave cloth, his face muffled in a head swath. Jesus told them, "Unwrap him and let him go!"

Not only does Jesus bring healing to the sick and dying, but he provides ample opportunities to involve people into the ministry, serving those around them who need assistance. Imagine bystanders acting on Jesus's command, rushing forward to pull away the pieces of grave cloths that kept Lazarus bound and immobilized. I have often thought upon reading this piece of scripture, time and again, how imaginatively this message can be interpreted in a contemporary setting. For instance, people who have been the repeated subject of taunting have been labeled with names that discredit them. It's as if they have sticky notes stuck on their foreheads with the offending names written on the note. Or they have strips of cloth tape wrapped around their chest with a disrespectful phrase stamped on them for everyone to see. The Lazarus story would be an excellent meditation or prayer expression. Imagine individuals wrapped in labeled cloths or strips of fabric being removed by helpful people upon Jesus' command, "Unwrap him/her and let them go!" In a way this scriptural command would be useful in our next story.

Labeling the football team

John is a big man. At six feet four inches tall and two hundred and thirty pounds with rugged good looks and gentle manners, he commands attention from friends and passersby in the rural farming community in which he lives and works. John is a stock broker working in a regional office for a national brokerage firm. He spends hours in his office talking to people, keeping track of stocks on his computer monitor, and phoning clients from a head set that suggests he is actually taking orders at McDonald's.

John grew up on a hay ranch run by his father and several other business partners. Haying can be a very profitable business. In a good spring and summer season their vast acreage could produce three cuttings of alfalfa for shipment to dairy farms in the region and an emerging international market in Japan. John knew every aspect of the business, but especially loved the growing season when he could be outside on the tractor cutting and bailing. When John was in junior high school he began to put on some size. Bucking one hundred and twenty five pound bales of alfalfa in the late summer sun tanned his body and defined his muscle mass. By the time John entered his Sophomore year in high school, the football coaches took note of his emerging physical presence and tracked him down as soon as school opened in the fall.

Five foot, eleven inches tall at the age of fifteen, John was linebacker material. But, because of his inexperience in playing football, he had trouble with the basics of his new position as well as the fundamentals of the game. "During practice on defense, I had trouble keeping track of the offensive movement of each play and who had the ball," John remembers. "I kept running all over the field trying to guess who had the ball instead of playing my position. My inexperience kept me in confusion much of the time, but provided ample opportunities for other more experienced players to tee off on me. Consequently I got caught in trapping positions, blind sided, and knocked down a lot. The coaches kept yelling at me and calling me off the field for more sideline instruction. The upperclassmen on the team thought I was a delightful diversion and began hassling me about my ineptitude."

"As the first game of the season against an important rival approached, the head coach had a special meeting with the players. He announced that each player would be given a name during the final week of workouts before the big Friday night rivalry took place. The coach indicated that he wanted to inspire his players, to be focused and aggressive. The name on each of their helmets would provide that special spirit to play at their hardest."

"In his left hand the head coach held a large roll of adhesive tape, the heavy kind of white tape the Red Cross recommended for wrapping bandages for severe injuries. In his right hand, the coach held a large, wide-nibbed laundry marker. As the players knelt around the coaching staff, one of the assistants took the roll from the coach and pulled at the loose end of the tape. The heavily glued tape made a ripping sound as it was separated from the roll. The coach pulled a pair of scissors from a duffel bag, cut the tape in a six inch strip and placed it on the front of the helmet of the nearest player. Then he wrote a word on the tape. When he stepped back from the player, the rest of the team leaned close to observe what the coach had written. The team began to laugh as the player took off his helmet to see the word "JUDY" written on the tape."

As the coaching staff successively pulled and cut strips of tape the head coach continued writing women's names across the front of each of the players helmets. John was one of the last members of the team to receive a name. When the tape was in place, the coach scribbled a short word across it. John removed his helmet to see the word "BETTY" in dark block letters. This opened an opportunity for a couple of the upperclassmen to continue their harassment aimed at John and his struggle to learn his position. One of them called out, "If you played football like you buck bales you'd be an all-league player by now." Peals of laughter rang out from the team as well as the coaches. The head coach returned to John and wrote another word on his piece of tape. As the laughter continued John gazed at his helmet to see the addition. "BETTY BALES" stared back at him. He was humiliated.

"The names were removed from our helmets as league play began," John recalled, "but my nickname stuck with me all season. Unfortunately we lost most of our games that season, so the female name gimmick to make us focused and aggressive turned out to be a joke. I got enough playing time and finally learned my linebacking position. The name calling continued from a few of the players however, and my humiliation at being called BETTY BALES continued from the first game to the last.

"At the end of the season as we turned in our football gear, some of the players grabbed me and forced me out to the practice field," John continued. "As punishment for being an underclassmen, I was taped to the goal post with duct tape. It was useless trying to struggle against so many of the team players as they wrapped me from chest to foot in glee. I was held firm, not able to move under the multiple wrappings that bound me. The final insult was applied as the players wrote words and statements all over the tape. After they admired their handy work they took some pictures of me in my immobilized state and left. The physical effect was claustrophobic, the mental effect was embarrassment."

"It didn't take long before word was passed around school that I was taped to the goal post. Before the principal and some faculty members arrived the same players that bound me came back to release me. With precision and speed the tape was cut in appropriate spots and pulled away from my body. As soon as the hazing stopped I began to feel some freedom from the stigma of the nick name that hung over me during the entire football season."

"As I continued to play football for the next two seasons the name BETTY BALES never came up again, I think in part, because I had grown to six feet two inches tall and was an all conference linebacker. On the other hand, using a woman's name to describe me represented disrespect to women as a whole and to me in particular. Although I didn't think of it that way at the time, I see it now as a very limiting way of expressing my self worth by someone attaching a label to me that is derisive and untrue."

John continued to work on his father's ranch each and every summer during high school and on through college. During the next summer after his Sophomore year he worked out a clever way of resolving the BETTY BALES nickname that brought him so much embarrassment and anger. "I took out my frustration on the bales of hay," John remembers. "To get in shape for football each season I would collect the bales out of the field the old fashioned way. I would walk the bale lines in the field with a driver and flat bed truck keeping pace with me. I was dressed in jeans and T- shirt, heavy boots, heavy leather apron, railroad gloves, and carrying two hay hooks.

As I approached each heavy bale I would lift the bale on its end, drive the hay hooks into the broad center of the bale, push the bale from underneath with my knee and lift it with the hooks and buck it onto the flatbed truck where a second man would stack the hay in place."

"In that repetitive manner I suddenly though of the coaches and players in the weight of each bale," John confided. As I came to each bale I would call out a coach or a players name, sink my hay hooks into the imagined person, lift the one hundred twenty five pound dead weight, and grunt out the words... I am not BETTY BALES, I am JOHN! This method of work went on for several days until I was sick and tired of lifting bales and calling out the names of those who labeled me. Soon the meaning of the procedure had worked its magic. It was a process of forgiveness and healing. In the physical energy of sweat, muscular energy and heavy breathing the pain of two disrespectful words left my body, mind and spirit. I was free to be me!"

CREATIVE MEDITATION IN THE GARDEN

I am acquainted with a woman named Judith who finds creative imagination in her garden. Surrounded by the inspiring and stately summer blooms of Delphiniums, Foxglove, Crocosmia, and Daylilies, she finds that her otherwise busy mind is emptied of all concerns. In the presence of brightly colored trumpeting blooms of Nicotiana, the umbrella blossoms of Johnson's Blue, or the low spreading mantel of Candytuft, she releases the problems of her working world into the bounty of her garden.

"It's amazing," she confides, "how the flowering world of nature provides such a calming effect. Consider, for instance, a neutral backdrop of leafy green Kinnikinnick. It doesn't seem too impressive, but it is immeasurably creative and adaptive. It provides dense cover, it's a good neutral backdrop to frame in a variety of flowering plants, the leaves turn rust colored in winter, holds soil on hillsides, and have small white or pink flowers that attract small birds. All the color and adaptability of Kinnikinnick or all other plants, for that matter, state their case without advertisement or fanfare. At least, I feel, not in a spoken sense. This is where the creative imagination of nature works its magic on me. In the quiet presentation of a flower I am taken out of my problems or the concerns of the day and transported within myself to appreciate the chromatic display before me. It's my moment of Zen!"

Judith is program director for a classical FM music station in the upper Midwest. The station's powerful outreach finds dedicated audiences both in the United States and Canada. "Creating interesting and varied programming for our listeners is a continual challenge," she confides, "a creative challenge I take very seriously! Sometimes the mental well runs dry trying to form new musical formats that keep our audiences happy. Then there are the occasional personnel problems that arise that need some micro-management. When solutions are not found and inter-personal skills fall short of their intended goals, I always turn to my garden for inspiration and creative imagination to find some answers."

"When I am turning soil, trimming plants, or simply appreciating the beauty of it all, my mind seems to unlock from the gridlock of trying to reason solutions out of problems that arise at work. The energy and attention I give to my garden is returned in kind by the natural order of growing plants and their quiet acquiescence of my presence in their natural environment. Stripped of the tension to find solutions at work, my mind is free to seek answers while I rummage around all the beautiful growing things. Strange as it seems, while I am concentrating on the physical activity of tending to plants and their welfare, a thought, an idea, a possibility, or an answer sparks my imagination and brings resolution to a work problem that I wasn't paying any attention to at the time. It is a process that I have used time and again with results that I owe a great deal to my flowering space!"

PROJECT: TANGRAM COLOR DESIGN *

Judith used her garden to resolve troubling issues and John used the open fields of the alfalfa ranch to rid himself of misused words that labeled him. Both used the natural environment to find creative imagination in their lives. Despite the time we've spent stripping away unhealthy labeling, we will use labels in the next design to help guide the participant through the initial sequence of development. The reason will become clear in a moment.

The design in question is a tangram. A tangram is a flat two dimensional Chinese puzzle made up of seven shapes – five triangles, one square, and one rhomboid. We're familiar with triangles and squares but a rhomboid may be a shape that requires some clarification. Webster's New College Dictionary defines rhomboid, taken from the Greek work *rhomboeides*, as a parallelogram in which the angles are oblique and adjacent sides are unequal. Classically, Chinese puzzles require disassembly and reassembly to challenge the mentally creative person. For those who have trouble remembering where each piece fits together (of which I am one) this type of puzzle can drive the participant crazy! So labeling becomes an important aspect in the development of this piece of work.

As in past projects, the materials needed are important, but become a bit more complex. One piece of heavy stock paper 6" square and a second piece of heavy stock paper 12" square are the main components to this assigned project. In addition to the paper a 2B pencil, eraser, ruler, scissors, and masking or drafting tape are needed. The design can be laid out on a table or a backing board, such as a thin piece of plywood or a drawing board. In addition, colored pencils, magic markers, watercolor or tempera paint and brushes may be used to define the shapes of the tangram into a completed color design pattern.

To get started, draw an X from corner to corner on the 6" piece of heavy stock using a ruler and and the 2B pencil. This will create four equal sized triangles. Next, at the top of the paper stock measure 3" across and make a small mark. On the right side of the paper measure 3" down and make a second mark. Line the two marks up with the ruler and draw a line. This will give you an additional smaller triangle in the upper right hand corner of the paper. Erase the line in the center of the triangle you have just created to make the triangle larger.

On the opposite side of the paper measure down 3" a second time and make a mark. Line the ruler up with the original mark at the top of the page and the new 3" mark on the left side of the paper. This time make a line than angles off to the left side of the paper. The line should not cross to the left hand mark but stop at the line that it would otherwise intersect. Illustrations one and two will give you visual guidance as you create your puzzle to this point.

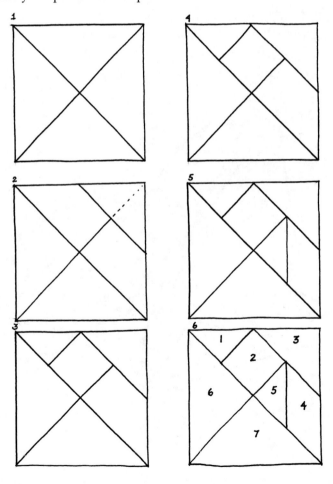

At this point in the design the participant should see on his or her paper two large triangles, one medium sized triangle, a small triangle, and a square. To finish the drawn design measure across the top right hand side of the paper and make a mark equally distant from the center of the paper to the upper right hand corner. Make a mark at 1 1/2" and a second mark at the bottom of the paper at 1 1/2" and draw a straight line from top to bottom. Erase the line in the upper right hand triangle and the bottom triangle, but retain the line in the center to form the rhomboid shape. You now have a complete tangram. Follow illustrations three and four for accuracy.

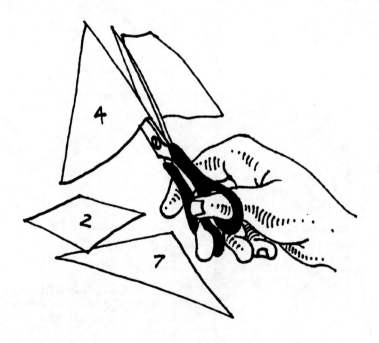

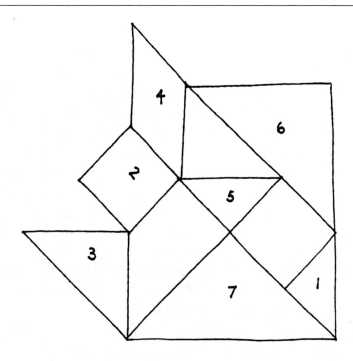

Take a careful look at your completed tangram design and make a mental note of the placement of the triangles, square, and rhomboid. Label each one of the shapes with your pencil as to size, or shape, or number sequence because the next step is to cut out the shapes. Once the shapes are cut out it could be a case of helter-skelter trying to get the design back into its original shape. A wise participant can always make a duplicate design to be safe, but for the more adventurous who thrive on Chinese puzzles, one design is enough!

Expansion and spatial quality become an important factor in this project. Placing the tangram shapes over the larger 12″ paper, the participant suddenly realizes his or her design shrinks in the larger space. So the challenge of this work is to expand the 6″ design to a new and different 12″ design using each numbered piece only once, making sure that all pieces touch at one point or another and that the entire new design makes contact with each edge of the 12" paper. Suddenly the origin of the tangram design becomes a stretched out freeform design that doesn't resemble the original creation at all.

In the Book of Genesis, God created reality out of chaos, but in this project each person is reforming reality and making chaos on a larger scale. That may seem disconcerting at first, but as the artistic creator, each participant can take the work one step further: make a design, pull the design apart, reshape the design in a different, larger, and better work. The same could be said for someone who is stuck with an old problem, business situation, or relationship issue: take the present situation, pull it apart piece-by-piece, arrange the components in a new way, and find a creative, workable solution. Perhaps working and concentrating on this design will help free the mind to bring resolution to personal difficulties in one's life or in the work place.

Don't be frustrated if all the tangram pieces have trouble reaching all four sides of the larger 12" piece of stock. Close counts! The idea is to arrange, rearrange, and rearrange again the pieces that create an interesting design while filling the space provided. With the pieces in place, outline the template shapes with the 2B pencil, then remove each piece to reveal your enlarged design. Quickly label each new shape with numbers so you don't lose the design with the background white space.

If you think the design looks anemic, too simple, or small on the enlarged paper increase your courage and creative power and make some additional lines that connect the original tangram pieces. Keep in mind that your eraser as well as the pencil lead can be helpful in eliminating line work as well as creating line work for a more complete design that meets with the participant's creative needs.

Finally, the project can be completed by using colored pencils or one of the quick drying painting mediums of tempera paint or acrylics to give the work definition.

The color will highlight the shapes but also define the background space, heightening the effect of balance, variation of shapes, and depth created by the use of contrasting colors. Once the initiate feels comfortable with this project and some imaginative juices are still flowing, erase all evidence of the labeling on the tangram and expand your consciousness to consider original tangram designs of your own choosing for future development. In the meantime, slide your tangram pieces all around with both hands. Can you put the original design back together?

*This project and three additional ones that appear in this book are taken from art resource manuals that I wrote called *Portfolio of Illustrated 4-Step Art Projects*, published by Prentice-Hall, The Center for Applied Research in Education, Inc., a division of Simon and Schuster. The series can be found in online book stores if you would like further clarification to these and other design projects.

Chapter Four

JESUS HEALS A CRIPPLED WOMAN

Now he was teaching in one of the synagogues on the sabbath. And just then there appeared a woman with a spirit that had crippled her for eighteen years. She was bent over and was quite unable to stand up straight. When Jesus saw her he called her over and said : Woman, you are set free from your ailment." When he laid hands on her, immediately she stood up straight and began praising God.
                                                            Luke 13: 10-13

If you've watched the movie, *Message in a Bottle* you may have noted a scene in which Kevin Costner, portraying a shipwright, is pulling a board out of a steam box used to bend planking to fit the shape of a sailboat hull under construction. Continual heat and moisture applied under steam pressure makes the fiber of the wood pliable so it can be bent into a desired shape, much like metal being shaped by extreme heat and tempered by extreme cold. Once the board is fitted and attached to the hull, it retains its curved shape and adds its pliant strength to the overall development of the vessel. However, because of the yielding nature of wood fiber, the plank could resume its original flat surface once the moisture vaporized if it's not fitted quickly to the skeletal framework of the hull. So bending and shaping of wood by a competent shipwright is a precise and delicately timed craft in the construction of wooden boat building.

Bending, shaping, and straightening is the subject found

in the Thirteenth Chapter of Luke, as Jesus has the opportunity to heal a crippled woman "with a spirit that had crippled her for eighteen years." (Luke 13: 10-17) To the frustration of the leader of the synagogue, Jesus is once again healing individuals on the sabbath. "There are six days on which work ought to be done; come on those days and be cured, and not on the sabbath," complains the Rabbi. (Luke 13: 14) The religious leaders of the day just couldn't get Jesus to keep regular office hours! But Jesus sets his opponents straight by calling them hypocrites with the rebuke,…"Does not each of you on the sabbath untie his ox or donkey from the manger, and lead it away to give it water? And ought not this woman, a daughter of Abraham whom Satan bound for eighteen long years, be set free from this bondage on the sabbath day?"(Luke 13: 15-16) The leaders, missing the opportunity to see compassion and healing taking place at any moment of any day of the week, are shamed by Jesus' comment and embarrassed by the crowd rejoicing at all the wonderful things Jesus was doing. (Luke 13: 17)

To gain some perspective on this Gospel lesson, I tried to imagine what it must be like for the crippled woman to be bent over at the waist. So I assumed a bent position and stood, walked, and attempted to function in a regular capacity while performing tasks in my painting and writing studio. To be limited to a small world view of the space in front of my feet presented not only a physical hazard, but a psychological one as well. I immediately felt the effect of diminished capacity. I lost my perspective in the studio as objects became obstacles, and seeing became strained.

The experience was an interesting sensation, but I didn't find the kind of sobering encounter the crippled women experienced because I conducted the experiment in the privacy of my studio, and I could stand up straight at any time. The crippled woman certainly endured public scrutiny, certain physical pain and limited mobility while I only played with the notion of deformity.

In the notes of the healing of the crippled woman, *The New Oxford Annotated Bible* states that, "This miraculous cure was unasked for by the woman or by anyone in her behalf." Regardless, the afflicted woman was present at the synagogue where Jesus was teaching and certainly knew of his healing powers, even though she may have been unable to see him from her bent and limited view. I would suggest that this woman had the kind of courage necessary to locate Jesus in the synagogue and perhaps find a way to draw his attention to her disability. It is the same kind of courage demonstrated in the Gospel of Matthew by the woman who suffered from hemorrhages for twelve years. 'Then suddenly a woman who had been suffering from hemorrhages for twelve years came up behind and touched the fringe of his cloak, for she said to herself, "If I only touch his cloak, I will be made well. Jesus turned, and seeing her he said, "Take heart, daughter; your faith has made you well." And instantly the woman was made well.' (Matthew 9: 20-22)

So how can we characterize a "spirit" that held this crippled woman in bondage for nearly twenty years? Particularly, what events precipitated her physical reshaping that confined her to a life of disfigurement? Jesus typically attributed physical disorders with the work of Satan, as exemplified by Jesus being tempted by the devil in the wilderness. (Matthew 4: 1-11) Satan tried to "bend" the will of Jesus three times in order to have him, "… fall down and worship me." (Matthew 4: 9)

It is well documented by biblical experts, and more recently by female theologians that control and subjugation was the lifestyle for a woman in biblical times. Jonathan Kirsch clarifies the role of women in his book, <u>The Harlot by the Side of the Road</u>.

> A woman in biblical times was expected to remain under the authority of a male at all times: as a child and a virginal young woman, she lived in her father's home until she married; once married, she lived with her husband and, she fervently hoped, bore and raised children; and, widowed, she relied on her own male children, who inherited their father's property. No other role was permitted. (p. 83)

And for a woman who found herself in a difficult situation such as seduction, intermarriage or illegitimacy her life took a tragic turn.

> ...(She) was shut away in the house of her father or perhaps one of her brothers, a spinster aunt with a dark past and no prospects, and she lived out her life in despair. (p. 84)

Perhaps the socioeconomic structure of the time contributed to the "spirit" that afflicted this woman. It's conceivable that words used against her may have acted like a steam box to soften her will and bend her into a depressed and misshapen form. Possibly cultural restraints held her in bondage, attached to a framework of oppression, eliminating her ability to choose a life for herself, weighed over with all the restrictions placed on her. Whatever her situation, our next story describes a contemporary woman caught in a cultural double bind that weighed heavily upon her body, mind, and spirit.

Trapped in a Cage

By all appearances Inez is a capable, productive, and outgoing person. She is a professional businesswoman who is the director of adult education programs for a well respected private university. Her outgoing and positive manner blends easily with the people she works with in a demanding academic environment. The creative way she has developed adult programs in off-campus community settings has brought her praise and recognition from students and peers alike. "I am always on the move," Inez explains, "and it seems like I spend half of my life on the freeway getting to outlying communities making sure the adult programs are running efficiently. I love my job and especially the students I meet. I feel a personal satisfaction to the creative programs I've helped develop and the positive reflection that it places on the university I work for."

But her business acumen was shaped out of a personal courage that defied a strong family and cultural background that tried to sabotage her desire to be an independent and creative person. Her story is a powerful statement of working through and escaping the kind of controlling language that would bend a person over in despair and defeat.

"Last year, I took a two week course designed to teach Spanish to adult students at an accelerated pace, "Inez begins. "Many of us had difficulty conjugating our verbs. As an attempt to encourage students to discern our limitations for learning a new language, our Spanish teacher told us a story of KeeKee."

KeeKee was a 2 year old baby chimpanzee who happily frolicked in the wild jungles of Africa. He felt the wind sweep his face as he swung from one tree onto another. He giggled and jumped with joy whenever he successfully played tricks on Mr.Lion.

One morning, KeeKee wandered into a clearing curiously discovering new terrain. Suddenly, he found himself mangled in a web of rope and vines barely able to move. Struggle as he may, he could not set himself free. Poor KeeKee had fallen into a trap set by hunters.

The hunters arrived, released him from the netting and placed him in a square contraption with bars on four sides. He attempted to squeeze through the bars but to no avail. Sadly, KeeKee fell asleep from exhaustion. He awakened many hours later.

Groggily, he walked ten paces forward and bumped into the bars; he walked ten paces backwards and bumped into bars. The same thing happened when he stepped to the right; then to the left. Poor sad KeeKee was caged in a zoo where he resided for 20 years.

One day, the zoo keeper approached KeeKee and informed him that he would have a new home. He was being sent to a place where he could freely roam and swing through the trees. Later that week, KeeKee was released from his cage and taken to his new home. He looked around at his surroundings. He saw branches full of leaves swaying from trees. He heard the gurgling of a nearby brook and the roar of a lion in a distance. KeeKee was free to frolic and to go discover this new land! But KeeKee slumped over and took ten paces forward then stopped; he took ten paces backward, then stopped. He took ten steps to the right; then ten steps to the left. He sighed and plopped down. Although the physical bars of his cage had disappeared, KeeKee subconsciously remained in his cage out of habit. He would not be freed from his cage until he allowed his mind to let go.

"Our teacher," Inez continues, "asked us to reflect on how our ingrained knowledge of the English language is caging our freedom to explore the Spanish language. Amazingly, once the barrier was recognized and broken, conjugating verbs came easily."

This story stayed with me and has challenged me to discern where I might subconsciously be caging my freedom to be fully alive. One area was an understanding of self based on feedback such as "You are not…therefore, you can't…"

"For example, I am a second generation Filipino American. From the dominant Western European culture, the feedback is "You are not white; therefore, you do not fit in." From the Filipino culture, the feedback is "You are not Filipino because you do not speak the dialect and are Americanized; therefore, you do not fit in." For a long time, I wondered what I was and where did I belong. I felt inept because I could not relate to the "back home" conversations of my parents and their friends. For me, home was here in the United States."

"My parents migrated from the Philippines post World War II and had faced many challenges while settling in a new country. They passed survival tips onto my brother and me such as "Avoid making mistakes or they will laugh at you." "Do not bring shame to the family--it is better to be silent." Although these words of advice were good intentions, it limited who I could be or what I could do because it created in me fear to risk being wrong in either culture, otherwise I would not be accepted."

"My cage was thinking I had to choose between two cultures. After many years of ministerial training and discernment, I eventually broke the barrier and learned to focus away from what I WAS NOT and embrace what I AM...someone who has a world of heritage and a world of residence and who belongs in both."

"My mother had old fashion notions regarding gender. Girls are to stay home and make babies; boys are to be the financial supporters of their families. Needless to say, I grew up in a double-standard household. I struggled with the feedback of "Why do you want to go to college and take business? You are not a man...it is better to learn to cook." When I finally earned my Bachelors in Business Administration, received an internship with the Federal government which eventually led me to upper level management position, I felt frustrated when my mother thought I became a lead secretary because "You are not a man; therefore, you can't be more than a secretary."

It is no wonder that as one of the few women managers at that time, I was driven in my work and internally I questioned my own merits without cause."

Inez continues her story. "My cage was my desire to convince my mother that I could be more than the stereotypical image of womanhood. I wanted her acknowledgement and acceptance of my potential as a woman. Until I received it, I was like the older KeeKee pacing 10 steps in four directions, unable to appreciate the fullness of his new surroundings."

"The barrier broke when I learned to contextualized my mother's experiences and view it from her perspective. She was a stay home mother and wife through most of her life-- as was my grandmother. She was content with her image of womanhood. Once I learned to respect her space, I was freer to live in mine."

"I am amazed at the numerous "You are not...therefore you can't" feedback that can cross our paths and debilitate our potential of being. "You are not a single male therefore you cannot be ordained as a priest. OR "You are not young, therefore, you cannot be interested in furthering your studies OR "You are not tall; therefore you cannot be a professional dancer." and on and on and on. In essence, such statements are discriminatory."

When Jesus saw her he called her over and said "Woman, you are set free from your ailment. (verse 12)

Like the woman with the spirit that crippled her, individuals who receive "You are not...therefore, you can't statements are bent over with shame, depression and eventually anger. Jesus brought joy to the crippled woman by acknowledging her presence. By touching her, he released her from her cage of limitations so that she might stand up straight. Inez concludes, "this Scripture passage encourages me to be healed and to be mindful of the words I use in all my relationships so that I may be a healing presence rather than a deterrence to their potential."

Project: Free Form Graph Design

This project is a further exploration of the graph design that was introduced in chapter one. I gave some very specific guidelines to the first design which was a way of keeping the initiate artist on a controlled, but steady course. That course of action was both helpful and yet a hindrance as well. A passage from the Gospel of John fits wonderfully here. "The thief comes only to steal and kill and destroy. I came that they may have life, and have it abundantly." (John 10: 10) I had mentioned the key statement in the first design was …'Although the design project in question is small in size it has the capacity for enlargement depending upon the adventurous nature of the designer.' Now is that time for adventure.

The first graph design could be looked at as the way of the Pharisee. Specific rules kept the design from breaking free of the specific number of squares. The design did provide some freedom of expression and an "ah-ha" experience was a real possibility, but strict limitation for freedom of exploration was missing. But Jesus speaks of an abundant life, a desire for each of us to be free from those who would steal our originality, kill our creativity, and destroy our will. So this advanced version of the graph design is built on the way of Jesus: no rules to trap the designer, no infringement on our capabilities that would bend us like a board in a steam box. With this design the restrictions are removed so that the participant, like KeeKee, can take more than 10 steps forward and 10 steps back.

You have already built momentum with the first static, symmetrical design, so freedom to explore a more modified, and asymmetrical concept will come about with less risk and more self assurance. Perhaps some novice designers have already expressed a representational drawing that goes beyond the rules set forth in the first project.

We return to the simple materials list for visual application to this project. The graph paper can remain the same size or can be represented with larger or smaller square units per square inch. To be really different larger and smaller graph papers can be cut into interesting shapes and used in the same advanced design. Graph paper of various sizes can be found at art supply stores, or appropriate software for computer usage can create interesting grid patterns and printed out as the basis of creative designs.

Once again a standard 2B pencil and Pink Pearl eraser are essential tools to use to inaugurate this enterprise. Some may want to advance beyond the colored pencil set to distinguish their work. Two companies make quality colored ink pens that give vivid and varied hues. Look for the Uni-Ball ink pen by Faber Castell, and the metal tipped color pen by Sanford. Use one or the other product, or mix both together, for some wild and impressive color combinations.

The guidelines for usage in the first project have now been broken and the rules-of-the-road that were established will now be reestablished by the whim and imaginative movement of the designer. So greater possibilities of "ah-ha" experiences are just beyond the movement of pencil and colored pen. This may be the best moment to take time to reflect on the written expressions of Parker Palmer before jumping into the unmarked but promising creative void. In his book, <u>TheActive Life; Wisdom for Work, Creativity, and Caring</u>, Mr. Palmer pins down the creative process.

> Work is action driven by external necessity or demand.... Creativity, in contrast, is driven more by inner choice than by outer demand. An act cannot be creative if it is not born of freedom. In creative action, our desire is not to "solve' or "succeed" or "survive" but to give birth to something new; we want, for a while, to be less creaturely and more like the creator. If work reveals something of our bondage to the world, creativity reveals something of how we transcend it

– and that fact gives rise to the dilemmas of creativity. (p. 9)

The original design developed in Chapter One was a prescribed series of unified square units set together to form one large pattern. Since all the units repeated the same design concept they are described as a symmetrical concept. The originality in this piece was formed in the first five-by-five square unit. The other three units simply repeated the original pattern while staying in the context of conformity. And conformity was the harmonizing quality the Pharisees looked for "to bend and shape" the world around them.

Now more freedom is called for to fit the expressive needs of the individual. Jesus, the radical restorer of human needs, calls forth the radical creative energy of the human soul and spirit to expand beyond the norm and into the co-creative realm.

Very truly, I tell you, the one who believes in me will also do the works that I do and, in fact, will do greater works than these… (John 14: 12) Now we look at the uneven quality of design, the irregular, the spontaneous formless shapes, pulled out of our imagination and made tangible.

To begin your project, take your original twenty five square unit design, developed from Chapter One, and use it as a starting point for the new production. It doesn't matter where you place the square unit design on the graph paper. Perhaps you could repeat the same design unit two more times but touching at individual corners instead of side-by-side. Or create an additional unit to be placed completely free from the other design units. The spatial quality of the graph paper will stand out much stronger as the random designs ramble across the paper in freeform fashion. Perhaps each square unit could have a different design, or some designs could be partially described, some could be in black and white, while others are detailed in color. There is more latitude offered here with freedom to explore, eventually leading to one, or several "ah-ha" experiences. The following illustrations will help visualize these artistic points.

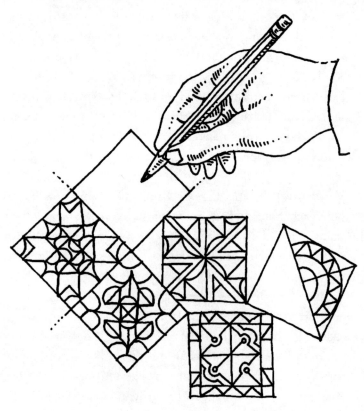

As the creative individual continues to develop imaginative graph shapes, design objectives are being woven into the project with consciousness and understanding. The most obvious principle that appears at this point is the development of a unique visual statement. Because there is freedom to explore layout possibilities there are many design shapes that are possible. One design may work, or all may work. Mature artists generally keep all their basic designs filed away in portfolios, drawers, and cabinets for future reference, to be dusted off at a later date, studied, refined, used in the same manner or used as a launching pad for designs of a different nature.

Finally, the objective that fits the character of this project can best be describes as the development of an interesting design project without a complete plan. Creative freedom doesn't always know where it is going. A minute ago the design wasn't there, five minutes from now it may be beyond the artists comprehension. What we have is the now-present-moment in which to be totally involved in the creative process and, moment-by-moment, enjoying the unfolding, unbending reality of the next visual revelation.

Chapter Five

LET THE CHILDREN COME TO ME

People were bringing even infants to him that he might touch them; and when the disciples saw it, they sternly ordered them not to do it. But Jesus called for them and said, "Let the little children come to me, and do not stop them; for it is such as these that the Kingdom of God belongs. Truly I tell you, whoever does not receive the Kingdom of God as a little child will never enter it."

Luke 18: 15-17

Recently I was browsing in a Christian bookstore when a large poster of Jesus caught my eye. The illustration depicted Jesus seated on a rock, holding a small infant on his lap, surrounded by children. Jesus was laughing, and the children seemed to be having a good time too. The artist's rendition seemed to visualize Luke's scripture story with considerable warmth and capriciousness. It's rare indeed to find a laughing Jesus in the Gospel texts, so the humorous attitude in the reproduced painting held my attention for quite some time. The Scripture passage from which the original painting was made doesn't suggest wit, however, but concern. Jesus has just reprimanded his disciples for trying to keep people from bringing their children to Christ's attention. (Luke 18: 15) But Jesus has a special place in his heart for the unblemished spirit of children. Jesus discloses his concern to all present when he states that…"it is such as these that the kingdom of God belongs." Then he drives his message home. "Truly I tell you, whoever does not receive the Kingdom of God as a little child will never enter it." (Luke 18: 16-17)

As usual Jesus goes right to the heart of the matter in this youthful story. It seems plausible that while Jesus is displaying fondness for children who otherwise wouldn't receive much attention, he has brought forth a clear lesson of trust through a chaste acceptance of God, but at the expense of his disciples. Jesus has a habit of creating dissimilar situations through the active movement of a paradox; while pleasing one group, he angers, or divides another. The longer I studied the poster the more my imaginative eye began to picture a wider view of the situation the painting might have portrayed. Taking liberty by enlarging the picture plane I visualized the possible contrast between Jesus and the children in a friendly and playful atmosphere, while in the background the Disciples could be described in a sullen mood-wary of being excluded from Jesus's attention to the children and embarrassed by the mistake they made. It could be suggested here that while Jesus accepts the innocence and openness of children, it could also be interpreted that adults are placed in a secondary role, segregated and alienated from a simple faith in God. As already noted in this book, much of the language of simple trust and creative possibilities are stolen from young individuals by their elders who possibly want to stop the simple message offered…"whoever does not receive the Kingdom of God as a little child will never enter it." Instead, more often, a child may hear…"Stop Acting Like A Child!"

However, the story of children being attended to by Jesus found in Luke are packed with goodness for children and adults. Clearly the simple message of assuming a childlike attitude was meant for the young and old alike. Jesus is delighted with children and those who keep a childlike attitude throughout their lives. Children have promise…they act freely…they are observant…they are vessels…they are ready to receive! Are not children a reflection of their parents, and do not parents see themselves in their sons and daughters? Thus the story summons us to a reliable homogeneity, an acquiescence to the presence and teachings of God. So that proclamation calls for some overprinting on the conceptual painting being played out in my mind while I gazed at the poster in the bookstore. A more credible painting would include parents and the Disciples gathered behind Jesus and the children enjoying the same freedom of expression.

It is difficult to find in the Gospels situations where laughter is described in the character and activities of Jesus. If read in a literal sense, the Gospel passages cast the Messiah as somber and serious. But if read imaginatively the text can reveal a Jesus who is full of character and depth, capable of showing a full range of emotions. With improvisation, laughter can be read into several instances of Scripture. Jesus' participation in the wedding at Cana might be an example. How could Jesus not laugh when the steward called the bridegroom and said to him, "Everyone serves the good wine first…But you have kept the good wine until now."(John 2: 10) The secret of water turned to wine is kept hidden by Jesus as he muses over the situation he created and laughter certainly was the result.

In the Beatitudes, Jesus demonstrates through his teachings all the blessings, warnings and behavioral conduct required for a better life, to a crowd hungry for change and healing. (Luke 6: 17-49) Sensing the emotional changes expressed by Jesus and the gathered multitude would not be difficult to visualize. His sermon informs the gathered crowd and his disciples..."Blessed are you who are poor, for yours is the Kingdom of God." (Luke 6: 20) Jesus exhibits visible warmth. "Blessed are you who are hungry now, for you will be filled." Jesus displays a broadening smile. "Blessed are you who weep now, for you will laugh. (Luke 6: 21) Jesus laughs and brings refreshment to those who have suffered and wept. So to the reader of this book: Look at the Gospels once again with a childlike openness and discover laughter in numerous passages in a human and humorous setting that may have been overlooked before. Here is some help. Imagine Zacchaeus, the tax collector, as a Danny DeVito look alike sitting in a tree waiting to see Jesus pass by and being called down by Christ because..." I must stay at your house today." (Luke 19: 5)

A Child's Story

In my neighborhood, as in most residential areas when school is in recess for the summer months, elementary school age children find ingenious ways to entertain themselves. Given colored chalk they take over the neighborhood creating original designs on driveways, sidewalks, and the curved pavement of cul-de-sacs. No cement surface is left untouched as they create large flower shapes, interesting animals, giant letters, endless variations of hopscotch games, stars, moons, rainbows, contours of themselves, and other shapes freely expressed that come to mind. Some designs wander from house to house suggesting that a unique tale is being told, started by one child and continued by another. All of this activity is accompanied by brisk chatter and occasional laughter. Observing parents standing on the sidelines and passersby understand and respect the creative efforts of the young artists and avoid walking on the colorful designs. Once the chalk creations are complete the children find other interests to pursue until the first summer rains arrive and wash the work away to reveal bare pavement for the next creative efforts.

The colored chalk the children use to create rudimentary hieroglyphics and representational patterns is an extension of their freedom of expression. The openness of their outdoor classroom gives them limitless possibilities to discover who they are when left alone to explore. As they tell a visual story on all the hard, flat surfaces that surround them, they explode with creativity because they are free of imposed directives: someone telling them how to perform, that what they are doing is wrong, or that they need to color inside the lines! It is the same innocence found in Mark's Gospel, as Jesus is perfectly happy to let the children be themselves and express their individuality through laughter. Two very visible qualities are demonstrated here in the self-directed chalk creations and in the painted poster presentation of Jesus and the children: pleasure and love. A strong measure of these commendable expressions have been demonstrated by Robert Grudin in his book, <u>The Grace of Great Things: Creativity and Innovation</u>, as he clarifies the effects of pleasure and love.

> Pleasure is the passive effect of beauty, the receptive sensation that, at the moment of insight or recognition, expresses itself, complete with adrenal burst, in wonder or laughter or tears. Love, on the other hand, is the active effect of beauty: the will to repeat or increase pleasure by participating in beauty as fully as possible. Thus the people who are most capable of

insight are most avid in their pursuit of chances to exercise it. (p. 59)

When children are left alone to exercise their creative energy, pleasure and love abound through insightful practice. Allowed their freedom to play artistically, children can perceive the true nature of their action independent of any reasoning process. In this manner, insight, through intuition, leads to ingenuity. Who better than children in their innocence can devise a clever and skillful creation? To be original, novel, and otherwise creatively self-reliant brings together the full strength of pleasure and love in action. The outward manifestation of children at play leads directly to that very capriciousness that was noted in the image of Christ surrounded by happy, laughing children. No one is threatened here. Pleasure, love and humor are intertwined, celebrated and appreciated for the time being, played out to the fullest for their season.

But as children with the full attention of Jesus, or youngsters describing a visual description with chalk, the fullest expression of what they are doing can move from a clearsighted image to oral modulation. Perhaps the interest expressed between Christ and the children can be noted as storytelling, Christ listening with his fullest attention as the children share their penetrating stories. To ask the neighborhood children what the meaning of their chalk creations delineates invites exuberant storytelling. In wide eyed expression a child's verbal description forms and shapes a healthy imagination necessary for creative expression. Their narrations are reflections of their inner identity in relation to their outer environment. It doesn't matter if the story is mythological, or truth. To a child, telling a story, and having an audience are paramount in developing personal character, a soulful spirit, and bringing meaning to their lives. These are the same mental and emotional qualities adults rely on for a creative, productive life.

One person who lived with "the child intact" all his life was comedian, author, musician, and television host, Steve Allen. He grew up with humor and storytelling by way of his vaudeville comedian parents, Bill Allen and Belle Montrose. Steve's father passed away when he was eighteen months old, but his mother continued to tour the circuits. Much of the vaudeville slapstick and on-the-spot-humor influenced Mr. Allen's creative thinking and set him up for variety shows designed for contemporary radio and television production.

Despite Steve Allen's exuberant comedic public image he was a man given to shyness and deep thought. The wonder of his creative life was a mystery to him. In the mid-eighties an interviewer asked Mr. Allen what was his secret to performing so many creative achievements. "I never asked myself that question," he replied. "It would be like asking how my hair grows. The mystery of creativity is just that: It is a mystery, and particularly mysterious to me about myself." Steve Allen died in October 2000, a fully realized renaissance man. He made 40 record albums, played the piano, as well as other musical instruments, wrote more than 4,000 songs, 40 books, and numerous comedic monologues. Encompassing his wonderful creative legacy, Steve Allen will often be remembered for his wonderful laugh. Amusement surrounded his thoughts and movements, and was just below the surface ready to be expressed at any given moment. That same energy can be seen in the freedom of expression of children who tell their stories in colored chalk on pavement, punctuated with laughter and chatter. Who will be the next Steven Allen, or Gilda Radner, Garrison Keillor, or Whoppie Goldberg?

Childhood stories can be told over and over until they are ingrained in our mind like a well used road map, unfolded time and again to reaffirm the imaginative course of our lives. Our next story is so ingenious and so full of life and humor that many who have heard the tale are skeptical as to its authenticity. Some think the story represents a false map that would have us believe in mythical buried treasure. But that is part of the fun of creative imagination in the telling of a story; we need myth just as much as we need reality. "Myths are narrative patterns that give significance to our existence," states Rollo May, in his book, <u>The Cry for Myth.</u> Others, however, believe in the truth of the story and are free to roam on their own memorable road map.

THE STORY OF "STINKY INKA"

Julie is a veterinarian in a small northwest community tucked in the folds of the foothills on the edge of the Willamette Valley where Christmas tree farms and dairies nestle side-by-side along the Cascade Mountains. Julie's parents operated a large Holstein dairy farm in the valley where Julie grew up learning to appreciate the pastoral, but hard working life, and the gentle nature of the cows in their dairy herd. When she turned eight years old she joined the local 4-H club with one promising Holstein heifer named Inka, given to her by her father that would serve as her first club project. Little did she know that her original animal would form the basis of her own herd and receive championship acclaim in milk production and as a competitive show animal. By the time Julie was a high school student Inka sired a small herd that grew to fifteen.

Inka's true name was Angeline Inka Monarch, a purebred Holstein Friesen bovine, with registration papers tracing her bloodline to the great Holstein Freisen herds of Wisconsin and the upper Midwest. "I spoiled Inka rotten," Julie remembers. "She was my baby, and after my daily farm chores were completed I spent the rest of my time seeing to her needs. I fed, watered and groomed her, kept her blanketed, her pen was immaculately clean, and I walked her daily; haltered to train her for arena exhibitions. When I got on the school bus in the morning Inka would follow me along the fence line, and when I got off the bus she would bawl for me to come and give her attention. Inka was smart. She knew how to open some of the pasture latch gates and escape along the fence line and walk into our front yard, ending up on our front porch, staring through the glass of the front door, looking for me."

Within two years of working together Julie and Inka had formed a loving connection. Inka had grown beyond her yearling and senior heifer age and was now a milk producer after giving birth to a set of twins, both healthy female calves. "Spring, summer, and early fall were the times for dairy exhibitions at local and state fairs," Julie continued. "Inka and I had formed a perfect bond, and in the show ring displayed before the dairy judge, we had a walking, stopping, and posing routine that was near to perfection. With me in my dress whites and Inka staged to show her classic lines we swept through the exhibition show rings of the spring dairy show and the mid summer fairs."

By early September Julie was back in school, but one fair remained to be attended. For the next two weeks the state fair was "the" annual classic event and the most important chance to show Inka with the best cows and their trainers from all across the state. Many people felt that Inka was the odds on favorite to take the championship in her class and Julie would be granted the grand showmanship award. Winning meant bragging rights for the remainder of the year until the spring dairy show gathered seven months hence. So during fair week Inka and Julie were among the participants who joined the immense number of 4-H clubs represented for the competition, with activities and displays found in the vast show barns on the fairgrounds.

"For two days Inka and I competed in preliminary show events leading to the best animals to be represented for the final competition on the third day. I remember those September days as being unusually hot in the arena and many of the handlers and their animals wilted under the repressive fall heat and lack of wind. Inka and I held up well despite the heat and we placed high in our class going into the final day's competition," Julie remembers.

At this point in the story Julie stops, smiles, and shakes her head, as the remarkable and humorously unbelievable story unfolds on the final day of competition. "On the final day I had washed, fluffed, clipped, and smoothed Inka's appearance to perfection. Two hours before the competition was to begin I fed Inka the customary bucketful of beet pulp. The beet pulp helps replenish an animal's natural shape. The feed also creates a thirst for water. When an animal drinks, the beet pulp absorbs the fluid and "fills out" the animals shape so that it achieves its best appearance as a dairy type for competition."

"Well," Julie continues with a broad smile on her face,

"Inka ate the beet pulp with relish as she usually does, but she refused to drink the water offered her. For some reason she didn't like the taste of the fairgrounds drinking water that day, and I went into a complete panic visualizing Inka in the judging arena looking like a deflated balloon! I coaxed her for an hour to drink but she refused. Near tears I turned around to see our veterinarian, who had accompanied our 4-H group to the fair, approach me with concern on his face. He could see that Inka had not taken water. With warmth and sensitivity, he told me not to worry, that he had an idea how to fill out Inka's dilapidated shape. He ran out of the show barn saying that he would return in fifteen minutes with the remedy."

"The vet returned at the prescribed time with a large grocery sack cradled under his arm. He put the sack down on a nearby bale of hay while I untied Inka from her stanchion and pulled her into the barn aisle way. To my surprise the veterinarian pulled three quarts of beer from the grocery sack. He popped the top from the first quart of beer while lifting Inka's head up by her halter. To my amazement he tipped the container of beer into Inka's mouth, massaging her neck and brisket as the liquid ran down her throat uninhibited. Without hesitation he repeated the same technique with the two remaining quarts. The empty quart bottles were quickly hidden in the grocery sack and deposited in a nearby garbage can."

"Inka just stood in place without showing much reaction. I stood in place as well shocked by what I had just witnessed! "Trust me" were the words the veterinarian whispered to me as he waved a towel near Inka's head to rid the area of the lingering beer smell. But within minutes the beer began to mix with the beet pulp and Inka's thin shape began to take showmanship form. Within fifteen minutes her transformation was complete. I barely had time to ponder the meaning of three quarts of beer poured into Inka's system when the loud speaker in the barn announced -first call to the arena- for the final class. I just had time enough to lead Inka out of the barn," Julie relates, trying to stifle her laughter. "I joined the remaining trainers and their cows already positioning themselves in the arena for the championship class. The day was just as hot as the previous two show days but Inka seemed in perfect form to compete in the championship round."

"All of the animals were led in a wide circle in the arena as the dairy judge stood in the center assessing their qualities as they moved around him. Since this was the championship round, the best-of-the-best, the judge was going to take his time, making sure that he positioned each animal in their correct position for the championship. Around and around we went slowly pacing ourselves and keeping our animals under control. Both trainers and animals began to feel the afternoon heat and it took some effort for all of us to keep alert and not let our animals lose their sharpness.

"As a ten year old I was somewhat shorter than Inka who was a full sized cow. My head was even with her head, and keeping her closely haltered, my face was close to her muzzle. Our eye contact and the gentle movement of the halter told Inka exactly what I wanted her to do; to stop, move, or pose in a certain way. I soon began to realize what three quarts of beer can do to a dairy animal. I noticed that Inka's eye lids began to droop. I was hoping the effect was caused by the heat of the day and nothing else. Suddenly she burped in my face and the combined beer and gastric odor about knocked me over. Small bubbles emerged from her nostrils and I reached for my handkerchief to wipe away the offending smell. No one noticed, thank God!," Julie mused.

"Keeping an eye on Inka and watching the judge for directions became a nerve racking exercise. Finally the judge was satisfied with his visual critique of each animal and pointed at me to position Inka in the center of the arena. That meant that Inka and I were in first place! In quick order the judge pointed in turn to each of the rest of the trainers and their cows to take the following positions until we formed a side-by-side line; first place to last place. The judge began to take his final view of each of the cows to make sure that the dairy strengths and breed ideals he saw at a distance, were the same under close scrutiny."

Julie pauses for a moment, laughing softly, before continuing her story. "I was elated that we were in first, and Inka never looked better. As the judge approached Inka I noticed that her eye lids were almost shut. She looked like she was going to sleep! I jerked on her halter chain to bring her to alertness but all it produced was a second belch followed by more bubbles and the offending gastric smell. I quickly wiped her nostrils as the judge moved along her side checking Inka's udder, pin bones, ribs, skin elasticity, and smoothness of coat. The judge approached and moved around the front of Inka gazing at her hoofs, brisket and head. He ran his hand over her shoulders, looked in Inka's ears, then turned and moved to the next animal in line. My heart was racing! Couldn't he smell the beer?"

"For the next fifteen minutes the judge went from one cow to the next satisfied that he had made the correct calculations in placing the animals in proper sequence. In that time Inka froze in place, her eyes were shut, her tail didn't twitch, she didn't even shiver the flies off her back. She was in the classic dairy pose so I relaxed my hold on the halter and stepped back hoping that the judge would notice how well trained she was, but also to get back from the offending smell emerging from Inka's nostrils. I took a moment to scan the audience who were watching the judging and found my parents conversing with the veterinarian. My father and the vet, their arms folded, were covering their faces with their hands, laughing softly, and staring at the ground. My mother stared at me, her mouth gaping in surprise. *He told them!* I could feel a flush of heat rush to my face as I tried to maintain my own composure. It suddenly seemed like hours that Inka and I stood before the judge, the other contestants, and the audience and I was anxious to end the judging."

"My thoughts were broken as I heard the judge begin his summation over the loudspeaker. As he spoke about each of the cows qualities, the reigning state dairy princess awarded the ribbons to the trainer of each cow. The dairy princess approached me last to award Inka with the grand championship! *Good*, I thought, *let's get out of here!* But the newspaper wanted a photograph. *Good, now we can go.* But the judge, my parents, the vet, and the dairy princess stood beside Inka for an additional photo taken by numerous 4-H members, farmers, and interested bystanders. *Please, please, I want to leave now.*"

"Finally, the cows were led out of the arena and back to the dairy barns. I gently shook the chain on Inka's halter but she didn't move forward. She stood frozen to the ground looking much like a statue of the ideal dairy cow. I pulled somewhat firmly on her halter but there was no reaction. She wasn't going anywhere. Frantically I looked around for my parents who approached with the vet. My dad went behind

Inka, twisted her tail up in a knot and pushed on her rump. Inka's eyes popped open and she stumbled forward. *Good, I thought, we're finally moving!* It was a slow process getting Inka back to her stanchion in the dairy barn. As we walked she continued her belching, leaving a trail of offending odor through the show ring and into the barn. People along the aisle way were treated to the smell as Inka passed by. *This is so embarrassing! People are sniffing and turning away with an awful look on their faces."*

"When I finally placed Inka in her stanchion and removed her halter, she lifted her tail and passed gas. Right before our eyes she deflated like a balloon. The flatulence drifted toward the rafters of the barn, out the vents, and into the fairgrounds. Inka dropped to her knees, followed by her hind legs, spending the rest of the day and night in a comfortable resting position. Occasionally, she would belch and pass gas, but her ordeal was over and she garnered the grand champion ribbon that hung proudly by her stall. I was proud of her and her achievement, knowing Inka didn't have to eat any more beet pulp, or especially, guzzle any more beer! From that day forward," Julie concluded, "she was called Stinky Inka!"

Telling a story is a way of being actively creative. It is also a way of marking time in our lives. Julie provided an important scene in her life that represented a benchmark of humor and warmth that is totally her experience; a memory to treasure always. A story is also a celebration which can be shared with others, added to their stories of similar situations, or not, which forms harmony and community.Ingenuity and imagination in the telling of a story often use the personal qualities of a fine actor: gesture, facial description, emphasis of a word or sentence, a pose, and emotional expression. All these qualities are added, like good seasoning, lending the story a wonderful and continuous flavor that never tires of being told, or heard. Our lives are reinforced as being important, and our memories sharpened by the telling of a story over and over again. Some may elaborate in the description of a narrative, but for the most part, it's very important to keep the account accurate for, "memories are made of this." Try changing the lines of a favorite story with your, or other children and you may be taken to task. "Hey," they will say, without hesitation, "That isn't the way the story goes!"

Project: A Spinning Kaleidoscope

It may seem appropriate here to suggest chalk drawings on your driveway as the next project. That certainly presents a creative next step, and I don't want to squash your freedom to explore in your own way. So stake your claim on the street nearest you and join the kids and draw your share of moons, stars, and imaginative shapes. To those who wish to stay inside, this next project will bring the same amount of pleasure and innovative surprises. We have talked throughout this chapter about "spinning yarns," anecdotal references for our ears. Now we will explore, as our next project, a circular color project that is guaranteed to describe a surprising visual account; a "spinning yarn" for the eyes.

I'm sure we have all experienced looking into the eye piece of a kaleidoscope tube, turning the cylinder so the colored glass pieces tumble into ever changing positions, creating sensory sensations that never repeat themselves. And I am equally sure that you have said to yourself, "I've found the perfect design, but there is no way to save it." Well now you have the chance, not only to create your own kaleidoscope, but to save the pattern as well, a design that is pleasing to the eye and contains a surprise ending.

The variegated project in question will be round in shape with eight evenly divided spaces containing one repeating design pattern, drawn first and finalized in an arrangement of water based acrylic colors. The visual effect of the completed craftsmanship suggests a well arranged, flat, but otherwise colorful pizza design! It is important to note that this endeavor is a bit more challenging than the previous projects, but it should not present a problem for those who have come this far through the stories and artistic enterprises concluding each chapter. Clear, step-by-step procedures and myriad illustrations will accompany this creative performance all along the way.

First, let's get your materials organized. A square piece of paper, about 10" or 12" in size is your first priority. Standard paper sheets are 8 1/2"X 11" in size. To make the standard sized paper fit this design arrangement requires cutting three inches off the long end of the sheet to make it square. An 8 1/2" square will be somewhat smaller, but will still work if you desire a smaller design to begin with. Larger paper can be found at an art store, in individual sheets, or ring binder book form. Add to the collection a simple compass, scissors, soft leaded drawing pencil (# 2 or 2B), eraser, ruler, drafting or masking tape, and assorted acrylic paints, water container, palette, and brushes. These have been the standard equipment for the previously assigned projects so they should be readily available.

Second, add these ingredients that are new to your basic supplies: A small jar of rubber cement or a large glue stick, a sheet of tracing paper, a piece of cardboard, (the same size as your 10" or 12" square piece of paper), and the most unusual item, a 1 5/8" panel board nail. For those who really get involved with this assignment a 10" or 12" piece of #300 illustration board can be substituted in place of the cardboard. The following illustration includes all the items found in the supply list.

To begin the project take the square piece of paper and fold it in half. (A) Next, fold the paper in half again, making sure the open ends of the paper are on one end and the creased folds are on the other end. The paper will form another, but smaller, square. (B) Fold the paper one last time, continuing to insure that the new teepee shape has all the open ends at the wide end of the folded paper that forms the base of the teepee shape. (C) Lay the teepee shaped paper flat on the cardboard and temporarily tape it in place. (D) Place the metal point of the compass at the tip of the paper, extend the compass pencil point to the open end of the paper edges and scribe a curved line along the base of the teepee. (E) Remove the tape from the folded paper and cut along the curved line and remove the excess scraps. Open the paper to reveal a circle divided into eight pie shapes. If the paper unfolds and falls apart in several pieces the folding process needs to be looked at again for accuracy. At this juncture the design in process will look like a big floppy disc.

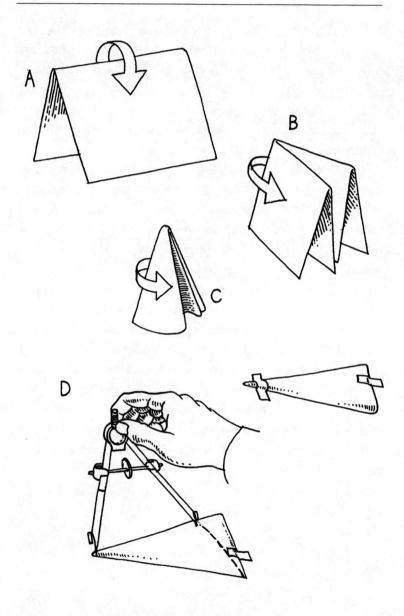

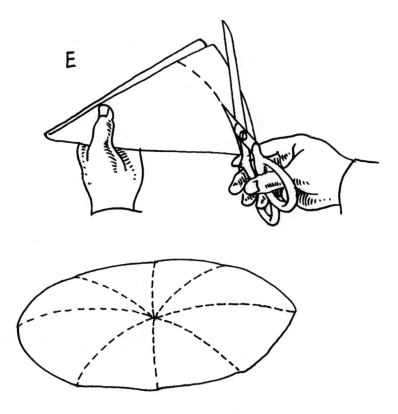

The pie shaped paper can be smoothed out on the cardboard base and taped in place. Use the soft leaded pencil and ruler to make dark lines over the crease marks to individualize each of the eight pie shapes created by the folding. Now the preliminary step-by-step manual labor is completed and active creative energy can begin. Choose one pie piece and begin to make some free form line shapes: straight lines, angled curved lines, circles, whatever comes to mind. Draw the design simply to begin with keeping in mind that the seven other pie shapes will receive the same design. (Illustration #1) When satisfied with the first design, take a piece of tracing paper that will fit over the design and tape it in place. Redraw the initial design on the tracing paper, remove the tape, and lift the tracing paper from the round paper disc. (Illustration #2)

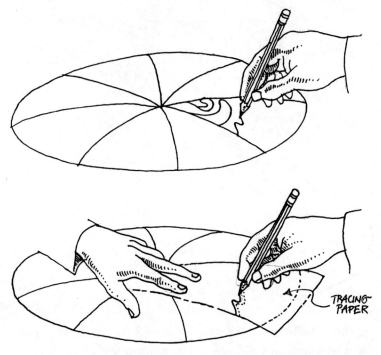

In order for the original design to be repeated seven more times it is necessary to have a light source to reflect the design on to the other pie shapes. Most people don't have access to a light table, but a window will do just as well. Tape the tracing paper line drawing to a window, making sure there is a strong light source on the opposite side of the glass to reflect the tracing paper image. Next, place the round paper shape over the tracing paper, fitting one of the individual pie shapes exactly over the tracing paper design. Tape the paper in place, draw the design, untape the paper and adjust it to the next empty pie shape over the tracing paper and redraw the next design. Repeat this pattern until all eight shapes have the original design drawn in. The design should look like a drawn replica of your favorite pizza; pepperoni, pineapple, olives, onions, tomatoes, extra cheese...the works! (Illustration #3)

Place the completed circular drawn pattern over the cardboard for a proper fitting. If need be, trace a line around the paper circle on to the cardboard. Remove the paper and cut the cardboard to match the paper. With the glue stick or the rubber cement, thoroughly apply a gummed surface to the cardboard surface (allow the glue to set up for a few moments) and place the paper circle down over the glue and smooth out the surface with your hand, or place a big book over the project. Let the project "cure" for awhile. Isn't it amazing how much an art project images a cooking recipe...and isn't cooking an act of creative energy? In culinary pursuits, as in art, we are in an operative undertaking of "cooking something up!"

In the meantime, take a separate piece of paper and experiment with some possible pleasing color combinations that can be used in your kaleidoscopic design. Remember color opposites work best for contrast and visual impact. Once you have satisfied creating and matching the color patterns for the design, begin to mix and apply the colors to your circular design. It might be a good idea to lightly indicate with your pencil where your colors will be placed on the individual shapes in each pie shape so you don't mistakenly paint a color in the wrong place. A design like this can be a visually confusing and sensory experience so it would be best to apply one color at a time on the areas indicated in each pie shape to avoid mistakes in painting. Follow the example of illustration #4.

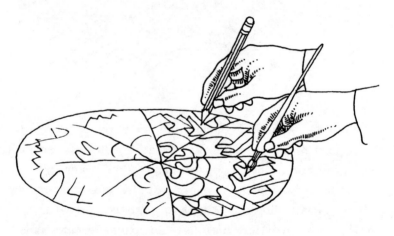

While most of the areas of the design can receive paint, some of the design patterns can remain the white of the paper. Contrast between colors can be enhanced by white spaces between colors and will heighten the effect of visual observation. Keep in mind that the color selections you are making have particular dissimilarities. The basic cool colors: green, blue, and purple, are considered opaque, are darker in appearance, and generally will cover a light surface in one coat. The basic warm colors: red, orange, and yellow, are warmer, transparent pigments that require two or more coats of application if you desire an opaque appearance in your design. I mention this because if you have marked on your design where a transparent color is to be placed, please erase the word before the light color is applied on the design. If you don't the word "yellow," or "red," or "orange," will appear through the color and can't be eliminated from the design. That is not particularly a problem for the darker opaque colors in your design selection.

Since the spinning kaleidoscope is an ambitious project, please take your time completing the color application. Water based colors tend to warp a thin sheet of paper, so the paper design mounted on cardboard should be enough support to keep the project flat. Earlier I mentioned #300 illustration board as a substitute for the support of your work. It is a thicker cardboard that can not only be used as a support, but can receive a drawn and painted design, eliminating the need for gluing one sheet of paper to a backing board. Cutting the illustration board however requires the use of an Exacto knife which compounds the difficulty of the project. I mention both choices of material so that you have a little more latitude in constructing your design.

With the completion of the painting you may feel that you are done with the experience. Now think back to the time when you looked through a kaleidoscope tube, turning the tube until the glass chips fell into a pleasing design. As long as you kept the tube still you gazed at the pleasing colored shapes as they remained in a static design. With the design that you have just completed on paper and cardboard you have, in a sense, the static design of your choice that you would have wanted to remain forever in the colorful tube. So what is the surprise ending I've mentioned at the beginning of this project?

The project is called a spinning kaleidoscope, which suggests that the design will have a moving function associated along with the aesthetics of the project. Once the colors have dried, take the metal point of your compass and poke a hole in your design in the center where all the pie shapes meet. Remove the compass point and insert the 1 5/8" panel board nail through the front of the design. The slightly flared head of the nail will fit snugly against the front of the design so it doesn't pull through the cardboard. Holding the nail from the back side leaves the project hinged like a car wheel to an axle. Please refer to illustration #5 as your visual guide.

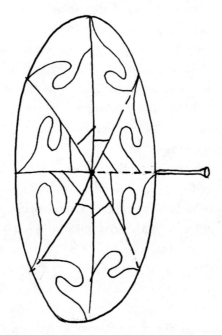

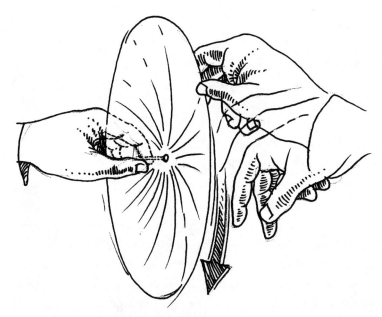

With the project held firmly by the nail from the backside, find a mirror and stand in front of it. With your free hand hold the curved edge of your design and give the work a hearty spin. As the design spins all the carefully planned shapes and color patterns melt together in a psychedelic maelstrom. The speed of the spinning circular design causes all the carefully planned design shapes and contrasting colors to blend together into unknown forms. Now the primary and secondary colors overlay each other to form compound colors, and the design forms reconfigure to create larger contours that emerge out of the eddying movement. As the spinning slows down other effects take place. Some colors separate, while other become neutralized. Some shapes seem to have a mind of their own, demonstrating a propensity to spin backwards while the overall design moves in the opposite direction. As the spinning continuously slows its rotation, other color combinations take hold and bloom like flowers in summertime, lasting a short time in their brilliance before their show is complete. This project holds so much promise and so many "ah-ha" experiences that it contains the same kind of slogan that a popular potato chip advertisement hawked.."Bet you can't eat just one!" In this case…" I bet you can't spin your kaleidoscope just once!"

Keeping in character with the telling of a story, the spinning kaleidoscope spins its own yarn with the varying changes taking place by the motion of the project. So the original design that was developed through conscious effort becomes a series of abstract forms that delight the eye, and inspire the mind. Go ahead, spin it again! Before you know it you will be showing the kaleidoscope to your friends and telling them about your creative visual story. Spin it again! Now you will be planning new stories through kaleidoscopic designs yet to be constructed.

Chapter Six

FORGIVE OTHERS THEIR TRESPASSES

For if you forgive others their trespasses, your heavenly Father will also forgive you; but if you do not forgive others, neither will your Father forgive your trespasses.

Matthew 6: 14-15

When my brothers and I were growing up in Seattle, we lived by Lake Washington, a lake twenty-two miles long that forms the eastern boundary of the city. In the early spring we gathered at the shoreline near our home and speculated at what the summer would be like. Not unlike a fidgety Labrador Retriever whining at the shoreline, we eyed the water with nervous anticipation. We thought of long, warm days and refreshing water, laying out in the sun all day, and cannonballing swimmers drying out on the park dock. We would take our shoes off and test the April water temperature in the hopes it would be warm enough for a preliminary swim. Only the very hardy on a double-dare would take time to swim to the dock and back, turning blue for their effort, but gaining important preseason bragging rights.

While we stood on the shoreline we always managed to find ways to entertain ourselves with the materials found on the beach. Like herons searching for food we would walk slowly, bent at the waist, looking for flat rocks to skip across the surface of the water. We challenged each other to see who could make their rock skip the most number of times while traveling the greatest distance across the lake. Like a major league pitcher, there was a manner of form and release that characterized good skip-rock throwing. With legs firmly planted in a semi-wide stance, while bent over at the waist, a swift side arm delivery parallel to the surface of the water would send the flat stone on its way. *Skip...skip....skip...skip... skip, skip,skip,skip. Plop!*

The combination of the flatness of the stone, its light weight, the velocity and angle of flight were important ingredients to the success of the skipping game. My older brother, the scientist/geologist, always found the best rocks to throw and held the record at 13 skips before it sank from the surface. It was a legendary throw, a thing of beauty! My younger brother, the attorney/judge, always disputed the record, mumbling something about the stone was moving too fast to be able to count that high. They argued at length over the throw while I, the artist/dreamer, could find beautiful rocks that never got higher than five skips before they splashed dramatically below the surface, disappearing quickly as if they had been dropped off the end of a diving board.

The challenge of the skipping game, of course, is to find and collect enough rocks to have as a reliable arsenal to keep the contest going. This requires a concentrated search to look for appropriate rocks that took us farther and farther down the beach. Considerable thought and concentration were needed when studying rocks for their ricocheting qualities, accepting some for their useful flight stability,while judging others as unacceptable for skipping. The rejected rocks, however, were stockpiled and saved for general throwing at a floating stick called bombardment, but that's another game entirely!

To many, drawing a parallel between skipping stones

and studying the Lord's Prayer found in the Sixth Chapter of Matthew might seem a bit nonsensical. Despite the strange analogy, rocks have a strength and quality not unlike the strength and quality of the prayer itself. Many references are made in the Bible attributing the use of the word rock to faith, stability, and determination. In the Old Testament, Hanna brings her child Samuel before the house of the Lord, praying, "There is no Holy One like the Lord, no one besides you; there is no Rock like our God." (1 Samuel 2: 2) In the Psalms, God's glory is proclaimed. "Let the words of my mouth and the meditation of my heart be acceptable to you, O Lord, my rock and my redeemer." (Psalm 19: 14) Upon Simon Peter's declaration that Jesus is the Messiah, Jesus responds by saying, "And I tell you, you are Peter, and on this rock I will build my church, and the gates of Hades will not prevail against it." (Matthew 16: 18)

The actual preface to the Lord's Prayer begins as Jesus addresses the crowds found at the beginning of Chapter Five. When Jesus saw the crowds, he went up the mountain; and after he sat down, his disciples came to him. Then he began to speak, and taught them,... (Matthew 5: 1-2). Thus begins a lengthy teaching of the Sermon on the Mount which is superimposed over the next two chapters of Matthew.

In the middle of Jesus' discourse he pays particular attention to the importance of prayer, advising the assemblage... "And whenever you pray, do not be like the hypocrites, but whenever you pray, go into your room and shut the door and pray to your Father who is in secret,...(Matthew 6: 5-6). Then Jesus makes it clear to the gathered multitude exactly how they should pray. This is where the metaphor of the skipping stones enters into the recitation of the Lord's Prayer. The flow of the prayer is broken down into simple one or two stanza statements that are easily recited and remembered. Reciting the Lord's Prayer, verse by verse, is like skipping words and sentences across the surface of our worship. When the prayer is complete, the weight of the petition sinks deeply into our faith. In this way we cast our trust and care on to God as our Creator believing that our petition has descended into the vastness of God's memory; to be held, remembered, addressed, and blessed on our behalf. So taking a prayerful stance and delivering our intersession our imaginary stone taps along in a consistent rhythm following the words of Jesus starting at verse 9 and ending at verse 13.

> Our Father in heaven,
> hallowed be your name. *Skip!*
> Your Kingdom come.
> Your will be done,
> on earth as it is in heaven. *Skip!*
> Give us this day our daily bread. *Skip!*
> And forgive us our debts,
> as we also have forgiven
> our debtors. *Skip!*
> And do not bring us to the time of trial,
> but rescue us from the evil one. *Skip! Plop!*

Stones, however, are not all the same size and shape and casting them upon the water doesn't always achieve the same result. Looking more closely at the Lord's Prayer we find different themes that guarantee varying results in each of the prayerful stanzas. For instance…"Our Father in heaven, hallowed be your name," is the first of five petitions found in the context of the prayer. "Our Father" is a sign of recognition. It is a belief that we recognize God as our Creator, and we will faithfully adhere to the remainder of the prayer that hinges on that declaration. That is an important basic skip!

"Your Kingdom come, your will be done, on earth as it is in heaven," is an admission of trust that God's Realm has been with us, is with us now, and we can rely upon the Creator's attention on our behalf in the future. Our metaphoric rock has skipped a second time.

"Give us this day our daily bread," is an expectation that we will be blessed with a variety of essentials: food, security, and comfort. It may also suggest a monetary blessing to be used wisely for ourselves, those close to us, the church, and for the betterment of others less fortunate than ourselves. And as creative people this verse can also indicate that bread is the fuel needed to energize, and activate our talents, not occasionally, but on a daily basis. And the skipping goes on!

"And forgive us our debts, as we also have forgiven our debtors," brings us to the central core of the Lord's Prayer. Here the direction of the petition changes focus. For the first and only time in the prayer, God makes a direct request of us. The verse starts off innocently enough as we request that God cancel our transgressions that we hold against others. However, the twelfth verse of the Lord's Prayer becomes more difficult to state because, in skimming across the surface of our prayer we run into a dilemma. At this point we must view our sailing rock in slow motion considering the seriousness of God's request and our response to it. For the majority of the prayer we rely upon God's support, but when it comes to forgiveness God is relying upon our sincerity, acting according to the honesty of our faith. The disparity here is that if we deny forgiveness to others for any reason then we cannot ask God's forgiveness for our own transgressions. Letting the sun set on our infractions holds us in bondage to our foolishness, hiding ourselves from our true nature and the creative world that awaits us.

The issue of forgiveness is so important in Jesus' explanation of the Lord's Prayer that He brings the issue up a second time for clarification before the assembled crowd. "For if you forgive others their trespasses, your heavenly father will also forgive you; but if you do not forgive others, neither will your Father forgive your trespasses. (Matthew 6: 14-15) Even the Apostle Paul reinforces the importance of forgiveness in his letters to the Ephesians and Colossians. "...and be kind to one another, tenderhearted, forgiving one another, as God in Christ has forgiven you."(Ephesians 4: 32) "Bear with one another and, if anyone has a complaint against another, forgive each other; just as the Lord has forgiven you, so you also must forgive. (Colossians 3: 13) With a number of scriptural passages emphasizing forgiveness, Jesus must have realized how much Christians would struggle with this issue.

Concerning the flow of the Lord's Prayer following the precept of honoring forgiveness begs the questions: Do the conditions and promises of the prayer become null and void if forgiveness is not exchanged? Is God controlling our habits and movements in punitive ways, or are we being led to freedom with an avenue toward a more abundant, creative life? Although the majority of the prayer is a reliance upon God's goodness, trust, and guardianship, in this instance, the weight of forgiving others their transgression is left up to us, not God. The issue is stated clearly and fairly. If you want my forgiveness, then forgive others their mistakes, sayeth the lord. It's as simple as that! It's as loving as that! So on this premise, our rock either sinks or continues its low level flight across our spiritual waters.

Finally, and most appropriately, the prayer comes to a conclusion that dovetails cleverly with the previous stanza concerning forgiveness. "And do not bring us to the time of trial, but rescue us from the evil one." Although this stanza covers a multitude of protective issues and safeguards the prayerful individual, it is also used as a reminder of what our life could be like if we do not clear up our transgressions. We could truly be trapped in a time of trial sensing confusion and pain that ostracizes our efforts to live a productive life because we cannot clear up issues with others that compound themselves the longer they are left to fester.

In many cases the thought out, and voiced appeal for forgiveness before God has a triangular effect. As we consider asking God to forgive our transgressions, extend ourselves to forgive another's actions against us, it is a good bet and a healthy idea to also consider forgiving ourselves for the pain and anxiety that has dwelt deep within our hearts and minds. As creative people we are diminished in many ways without forgiveness acting as our illumination. Much like a three way light bulb, we function on the lowest level of light in our personal and productive lives. But full exoneration allows us to turn the three way bulb up to its highest brilliance allowing each of us the opportunity to act that, as Robert Gruden suggests in his book, <u>The Grace of Great Things</u> ..."the liberated imagination is a limitless faculty, heroically capable of redeeming life and renewing the world." (p. 50).

The next narrative conveys a man's unforgiving nature that colored his whole life for a number of years until a synchronistic event changed his life and illuminated his path on the way to becoming a freer and more creative person.

"You Look Like a Chicken with Your Head Cut Off"

Roger is a man who loves mathematical figures. As a certified public accountant he is sole owner of an accounting firm in his home town, a growing community blessed with a variety of thriving agricultural and biotechnical businesses, and anchored by a major land grant university located a comfortable distance from a large metropolitan area in the state in which he works.

His clients think the world of him for his thorough and accurate tax work and for his skills as a certified financial planner. They trust his work and confidentiality explicitly but, on occasion, will admit that they worry about his work ethic. Clients have expressed that Roger seems to be driven in his work beyond the norm, worrying constantly, checking and double-checking every account making sure that he hadn't made any mistakes. Similarly, during tax season, his employees were quite often driven to distraction by his serious demeanor and fastidiousness, checking thoroughly each account for errors.

Roger admits to being distracted from fully enjoying his work but couldn't placate a malaise he felt within himself. "Many times during the long and difficult tax work I perform I felt like someone was eavesdropping over my shoulder, keeping an eye on the quality control of my business performance," he confides. "I really couldn't understand this unsettling feeling I had until a recent incident in a grocery store changed, not only my business practices, but how I relate to my clients. The incident had much to do with what I thought was an act of cruelty enacted against me by a teacher in elementary school nearly thirty years previously."

"Recently while I was shopping at the local supermarket, deep in thought as I surveyed the fruit in the produce department, I was approached by an elderly man who looked somewhat familiar to me. He hailed me by my first name, and when he saw the puzzled expression on my face, he introduced himself as Mr. Benoit, my former sixth grade elementary school teacher. I hesitated for a moment, collecting my demeanor, trying to place Mr. Benoit in a chronological context of my school age memories. As we exchanged greetings and began a grocery cart conversation, I was suddenly thrust back into my sixth grade classroom, rummaging around a compact room located on the third floor of a very old red brick school building located within walking distance of my home. In the middle of our conversation I focused on his voice inflections and mannerisms that suddenly brought back reminders of a painful incident that took place between us in that old classroom those many years ago."

"Without much effort, my memory swept me back into that classroom with its tight rows of desks, squirming students, and squeaky wooden floor. Everyone in the classroom thought Mt. Benoit had a hearing problem because he talked so loud, barking out instructions like a Marine Corps sergeant. His voice carried so well, students in classrooms at the other end of the hall could hear him teaching our class. He organized the class and taught as if every student was on the same learning level, and he had little patience with those who couldn't keep pace with the rest of the class. We all moved in block formation; no standouts, and no one falling behind."

Roger is quiet for a moment before continuing. He leans back in his office chair, surveys his desk of client's files and tax code books, stares at the moving screen saver pattern on his computer, takes a deep breath and continues his story. "The experience of my entire sixth grade year is shaped by one incident in that classroom. What I remember of my educational experience that school year was encapsulated in that single day. The day in question had a fuzzy, out of focus kind of peripheral vision to it. The experience was so intense that tunnel vision is how I would best describe my view of the pain I felt."

"Mr. Benoit was teaching a math unit that day, an exercise I always looked forward to because I felt math was one of my stronger areas of study. He sent us, one row at a time, to the blackboard to write down several number combinations to be added together with our answers chalked out at the bottom of the sequences. Even as a child I was demanding in my calculations, always adding my numbers together by tapping the chalk next to each number. This method left little dots next to the columns that resembled a coded system resembling a series of small snow flakes. It wasn't a fast method of adding, but it always worked for me. Unfortunately, my slowness at the blackboard that day got me into difficulty."

"I sensed that the other students from my row had completed their work at the blackboard and were waiting for me to finish. I remember how quiet the room seemed and how the sound of my tapping method of adding seemed to intensify in volume the longer I worked at the figures. Beads of perspiration marked my forehead, and I could sense the eyes of the entire classroom burning a hole in my back. I hesitated for a moment as I lost count in one of the columns of numbers.

I could hear Mr. Benoit pacing in the back of the room as I started to recount the numbered column from the top. Sweat was now running down the middle of my spine in a single rivulet as the experience of standing in front of the entire class seemed to drag on forever. As I finally neared the completion of the addition problem, Mr, Benoit's patience ran out. With his characteristic loud, piercing voice he stated his displeasure with my progress. 'What's the matter, Roger' he said, 'you look like a chicken with it head cut off!'

"With the thought of looking like a headless chicken, I froze in place at the blackboard unable to finish my rudimentary calculations. Mr. Benoit told my row to return to their seats, commanding the next row to take their place at the blackboard. I felt embarrassed as I walked the short distance to my seat. I tried not to look at other students, but my recollection of the situation seemed to indicate that many of the students were not concerned with me, but with their own math skills as they took their turn at the blackboard in front of the classroom. The whole class was tense, fearful that Mr. Benoit would use an equally derogatory remark against any one of them who failed to meet his time allotment for adding figures."

Time has erased much of Roger's recollection of any further feelings following that dramatic school day. He admits to feeling traumatized by Mr. Benoit's abusive remark, for it registers in his memory as if it happened only yesterday. Roger moved on however, considering the incident closed, glad to have escaped the harsh reality of a teacher lacking sensitivity and effective teaching skills. It's the side effects of being labeled as a "headless chicken" in front of his peers that limited his creative abilities in mathematics and plagued him into the next level of school.

"I do remember in the three years following my sixth grade experience I shied away from taking additional math courses in junior high school, and avoided volunteering information openly in math classes I was required to take," Roger continues. "However, by the time I entered high school, I seemed to be back on track taking advanced math classes, focusing on calculations and formulas that captured my imagination. I put Mr. Benoit out of my mind, or so I thought, until we crossed paths in the produce department of the supermarket."

"I had focused so hard on my schoolroom memory that I momentarily lost the thread of my conversation with Mr. Benoit in the supermarket. "I'm sorry, what did you say?," I found myself asking. "I asked if you are still an accountant in town?," replied Mr. Benoit. Coming back to full attention I replied that my business was nearby, that I was quite busy with annual tax work and conducting financial planning seminars for my clients. He seemed pleased with my success and briefly reminisced about his teaching career and how he is enjoying his retirement."

"As he continued to speak I became aware that Mr. Benoit had no idea how his remarks hurt me in his sixth grade classroom. Therefore, he would not be aware of the resentment I held against him. Suddenly, the weight of judgment I held against Mr. Benoit for all those years, and his unawareness of any wrong doing on his part became a burden I needed to let go of. So as we continued to talk, leaning on our shopping carts, staring at the varieties of apples and oranges, I silently forgave my old teacher his trespasses, and in turn, asked God to forgive the grievance I held against my former teacher," Roger confessed.

Forgiving his former teacher gave Roger fresh eyes to see the man in front of him as a real person, an aging man who lasted through a thirty year teaching career with many positive days of teaching to be sure, and some bad ones too. Now Roger could identify with his former teacher as a peer, no longer as a student. In forgiving Mr.Benoit, Roger could understand and lay aside his former teacher's faults as he suddenly realized his own faults for placing unnecessary burdens and stress on himself, and his employees. Roger felt there was genuine regard for each other as they ended their conversation and parted amicably, all silently witnessed by the congregation of polished apples and shiny plump oranges.

"I stood in front of the apples for some time seeing a smeared vision of muted red through the tears in my eyes, considering what a blessing took place between Mr. Benoit and me," Roger confessed. "In the days to come, I worked without an accompanying malaise, the feeling that someone was eavesdropping behind me. I had the distinct feeling that the act of forgiveness canceled the fear of Mr. Benoit's words and took away the burden of performance dictated by the behind the back taunt – You look Like a Chicken With Its Head Cut Off! I still give as much attention to detail for my clients and their tax work, but the tension in the office is, for the most part, gone." The final surprise came recently when Mr. Benoit showed up in my office with a bulging file folder of papers, asking my secretary if he could see me for tax work. After thirty years his voice still carries," Roger mused.

The descriptive use of water and rock forms returns once more to our narrative, as natural elements play an active part in the action of forgiveness. In a steep, high alpine meadow, a large waterfall cascades down an overhanging rocky mountain face. The solid water mass tumbles from above breaking into thousands of sparkling, misty droplets on its descent to the rocks below. A deafening roar of release is created as the water sprays in all directions, and a rainbow dances along the surface of the moving curtain of water. The act of forgiving can have that same freeing release of refreshment, freedom, and celebration. Perhaps Roger felt a similar release as his eyes filled with tears, standing transfixed in the aisle at the supermarket. All the pent up emotion and tension held against another person quite often is released in a similar manner within the body: tears flow, the mind is cleared, the body relaxes, the breath exhales, and the voice proclaims!

In other instances, forgiveness may take the form of a slow time release like ripples of surface water pushed by a gentle wind to meet the shore in a continuous, gentle motion. This slow release is reflected in a traumatic incident a woman friend was experiencing. She was going through a difficult divorce and held many grievances against her former husband. So strong were her feelings against him that it was affecting her physical and emotional well being. In counseling, her therapist suggested that she find an appropriate object to cast her unforgiving feelings onto. She decided on a round rock that was the size of her palm and, over time, and through careful therapy she placed all the grievances and unforgiving anger against her former husband on the rock. At the end of her counseling she and the therapist performed a small ceremony at a nearby lake. Holding the rock between them, they prayed briefly for forgiveness, and, in turn, to be forgiven. Afterward, the woman hoisted the stone and threw it as far as she could into the lake. The scapegoating effect helped her release her feelings constructively, cleansing her past transgressions, signaling the beginning of her healing process.

Sometimes the act of forgiveness is more subtle, acted out by individuals who find creative avenues on their way to change. Some of the stories described in this book contain elements of forgiveness that settle differences without the clear evidence of the Lord's Prayer being used as a guide. In chapter four, Inez desired to have her mother, who lived out of a different cultural model, accept Inez's potential as a woman stepping beyond her mother's barrier that stereotyped her image of womanhood. Once Inez recognized her mother's contentment to live within the confines of her cultural modes, learning to respect her point of view, she was free to live in her own space. In this respect, Inez was able to look at the hurtful incident with her mother as the protagonist, put events it proper perspective, seeing it from the other person's point of view, and neutralize the tension between them.

John, who suffered being labeled as "Betty Bales" by his football coach, discovered a unique way to exercise his act of forgiveness through physical labor. By hooking and lifting heavy bales of hay, day after day, voicing his real name over the prescribed derogatory remark he diminished and eventually erased the harmful effect the words had over him. He empowered himself through exhaustive physical labor beyond the point of feeling the pain of being labeled and sensed the release within himself to be a free person of his own choosing. He was able to move from blame to acceptance, acceptance to freedom, and get on with his life.

What Roger and the woman experienced in their shared stories is the cleansing aspect of the act of forgiveness. While they didn't recite the Lord's Prayer to the rhythm of skipping flat stones they, none the less, found creative ways to forgive past painful experiences that limited their full participation as the creative people they wanted to be.

Roger may never look at the produce department in quite the same way again, and the woman will certainly find, standing at the lakeshore, a strange dichotomy of painful remembrances mixed with the wholesome healing of her memories, a life giving experience. Fitting the context of the theme of this book, all these examples can be a creative work, a conceptual "ah-ha" experience because each person is empty of guilty feelings and anger ready to be filled with new energy and self directed creative expressions.

Projects: A Holding Stone And A Rub Stick

Much attention has been focused on rock and water symbols as a metaphor for describing strength and stability within an individual's faith structure that demonstrates the effectiveness of forgiveness and freedom. Turning to nature to find new imaginative forms for visual expression, therefore, seems most appropriate at the conclusion of this chapter. I have included two projects to contend with that have a suggestive theme in mind; creating a work of art that brings memories to light, both painful and joyful remembrance of past experiences, or for things hoped for in the future. In that context, the first project centers around the simple development of painting on a rock. It can be called a "holding stone,"or a "memory rock." In reality, the person painting on the rock can create the symbols and shapes, and give each stone a name uniquely their own.

I Can't Draw A Straight Line With A Ruler

The second project is created by carving and sanding on a small block of soft wood, which can be described as a "rub stick." The projects not only serve as visual art pieces, but can be held in the hands to be rubbed and stroked adding sensual pleasure to the experience of each project. As you will soon discover, we are no longer dealing with flat two-dimensional surfaces of height and width, but three-dimensional forms of height, width, and depth, objects with volume and weight.

To begin this project I need to set the scene with a short story. Recently I was visiting friends at a popular west coast ocean beach. As we walked along a sandy trail on our way to the water, two women were seated nearby with a collection of flat beach rocks arranged carefully around them. The rocks had a variety of simple scenes painted across their smooth surfaces: beach scenes, creative symbols, dancing human figures, sea creatures, waves, birds, trees, boats, lighthouses, kites, religious symbols, and the like. The women were continuously painting on new rocks, hardly aware that we were watching their creative efforts. My friends looked briefly at their work and moved on toward the beach. I, on the other hand, stuck around.

What I observed of their creative expression was a very simple, pleasurable activity that requires very little effort. The rocks were selected for their relative size, each fitting comfortably in the palm of my hand. Their weight was not excessive and their shape was flat on both sides with soft rounded edges of about a half inch or so. The rocks were selected from the tide line where the surf continuously wore the stones to a smooth surface. The two women carefully prepared each stone by washing each one in fresh water to rid their surface of sea salt and set them aside to dry in the sun. Without any other preparation they drew whatever came to mind on each stone with pastel crayons.

The women's free expressions developed on one side of a stone, were occasionally painted on both sides of another stone. Once several colors were added and they were satisfied with the results, a coat of matte spray fixative was applied to the surface design to ensure the pastel colors would not be rubbed off. Once the spray fixative dried the pastel colors showed up beautifully. That's all there was to the completion of the work!

I liked the designs so much, that after careful consideration, I bought a couple of the painted rocks, much to the delight of the two women. I placed the rocks in my painting studio where they lend their symbolism and remembrances among other items I have collected.

These two proposed projects, the "holding rock" and "rub stick," present some changes in the format of artistic enterprises introduced so far. The safety of the flat graph paper lines, present in two previous projects, is no longer present as a guide to rely upon for creative work. Working on a raised surface may intimidate and limit freedom of expression because of the rock and wood's irregular shape and raised surface. Another factor limiting the novice draftsperson's freedom is the lingering voice of not being able to draw a straight line with a ruler, the idea that without draft paper lines, small square units, the use of an eraser, and painting within the lines; they are hesitant to start on a free form design on a elevated surface. These apprehensions are understandable.

If you have come this far through the book, trying each of the flat two-dimensional projects with some success, then perhaps you have built enough confidence in yourself to take the next step creatively. So let's look at some of the positives of three dimensional creations. To start with, the stone can be looked at as a fat piece of paper! Just because the shape of the object has depth doesn't mean you can't work on the top and bottom areas which are relatively flat surfaces. Consider also that the stone and block of wood, considered for this project, are small enough to fit in the palm of your hand. That means any designs to be applied to the natural elements will be small and intimate. Since there are no art standards of excellence to adhere to in any of the projects, the budding creative person is free to express themselves through artistic means without the lingering thought that they have to perform to the standards someone else imposes as good and acceptable.

Getting started may take some time. If you are hesitant to create with pastels because you can't think of shapes to apply on the rock surface, consider the chalk drawings children develop on sidewalks mentioned in chapter five. Their designs are very elemental, simple, and free. They work without hesitation creating imaginary, as well as realistic, forms visualized in their head and reinterpreted on pavement, without consideration for art principals and realistic accuracy. Take this as a place to start. If ideas don't come right away, take a piece of paper and pencil and experiment by drawing creative shapes that you might find in a design book in the library. Use your natural surroundings and repeat shapes of flowers and trees, the swirl of clouds, the flight of a bird or kite flying high. Anything to get you started and your juices flowing. If you find the drawings you've made on paper satisfactory, then you have the basis for transferring the shapes to the stone surface.

The designs created on the two stones that I purchased

from the women at the beach are some very primitive pastel shapes. On one stone, a line drawing of a head is represented by a round circle, hair is described as short straight lines radiating out from the circle, like the rays of the sun. The face is developed with two circles for eyes and a straight line for the mouth. The neck is formed from two straight lines at the base of the head shape that meet a long curved line representing raised arms at the end of either side of the line with three lines extended for hands. On the opposite side of the rock is two additional designs of similar fashion. Simple but expressive! See the following illustration.

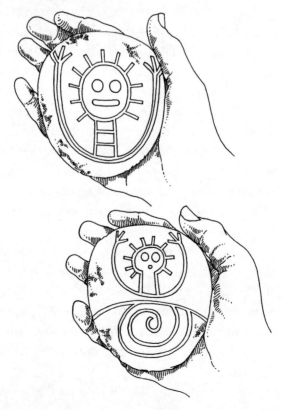

This would be a good place to stop and consider materials needed for the project and mention where rocks may be found. Along many scenic ocean beaches environmental concerns and shoreline management legislation have halted the collection of natural material that denude the beaches of their charm and beauty. There is also the consideration that many people don't live in the vicinity of ocean beaches where quality rocks may be located. In that case landscaping companies who can be found in the yellow pages of a telephone book, provide rock material including river rock, which is a great substitute for ocean rock, to use for your painting project. In some cases varied rock shapes have popped up in garden plots, along road sides and new construction sites. As for pastels, whether in pencil or stick form, and matte spray fixative, you simply need to go to your nearest art supply store for those materials.

Now that you have considered a rock to paint on, the next consideration is color. Not only will you be applying color to the stone surface, but you must regard the coloration of the existing surface. Most common rocks are a light gray or muted black, warmed with an accent of pale orange or white flecks throughout the surface of the stone. Most of us are used to beginning with a white surface, whether writing a letter or painting on a canvas, so the darker surface may intimidate the first time rock painter. Surprisingly, most colors work well on a stone's darker surface. The cool color ranges of green, blue, and purple stand out well together, as do most of the warm color ranges, especially pink and red. Gray and white work well as wide outlines by themselves or used between bright color pattern development.

In applying the pastel colors it is important to keep your

hands away from the color, because fingers holding the stone steady may smear the pastels before the fixative is applied. Once all the colors are completed, place the rock on a paper towel or piece of cardboard. Hold the spray fixative six to eight inches from the rock and spray your design with a back and forth motion for a brief moment. Wait for the fixative to dry and check to see what changes the application has made to your work. Generally the spray will even out the color, giving the surface a slight shine and brilliance. Touch the surface of the pastel paint. If it comes off on your hand, give the work a quick second spray to finally seal the color. Avoid overspraying because the colors may run or blotch together ruining your visual effect. Set the rock aside to thoroughly "cure" and work on another rock at your leisure. As you work, think of the fun places you could put your rock painting projects: on book shelves, on the kitchen counter, in a clear bowl of water in the bathroom, in the garden or on the porch steps. Wherever your imagination decides to place them!

Now we turn to the "rub stick" which has been a popular creative subject for many people. Imaginative individuals have taken on the task of shaping pieces of wood into carved objects by whittling. Others have shaped long tree branches into walking sticks with images adorning their curved surfaces. Some people have collected driftwood to be placed in their yards to make a visual landscaping statement. But a rub stick, or a "handie," as some people describe it, is developed for more sensual handling in the hands of the creative person.

Small wood pieces of soft pine or fir are appropriate for this project. The desired dimensions for a piece of wood that fits comfortably in your hand would be 2" X 2" X 5". Consulting a lumber yard for the material is your best bet. Perhaps some already cut scraps will be available without the need to buy a long piece of wood that won't be used. The lumber yard would also provide you with some rough surface sandpaper, as well as fine textured sandpaper for finish work.

Creating a rub stick is meant to be a project that is developed over time. The pleasure of shaping the wood with a variety of sandpaper takes the creative person on a journey of touch, movement, and memory. The constant motion of sandpaper crossing over wood grain is a slow shaping process. The rhythm of the action is like a mantra, a slow repetitive movement that calms the heart but awakens the spirit. The theme of rhythm is reminiscent of Danial-san, the young karate student under the care of Mr. Miagi in the film, *The Karate Kid*. In order for Daniel to learn the basics of hand and arm movement characteristic of the revered oriental discipline, he had to wax all of Mr. Miagi's cars as part of his first training lesson. The method was, wax on…wax off! It was a clever scene in an otherwise predictable movie that demonstrated a way to learn hand and eye coordination through repetitive motions. Sanding wood can have a similar effect.

Some creative individuals need a plan to give them direction on their wood piece, while others prefer to begin unimpeded by intention. Planned lines can be drawn on the small piece of wood to define the four individual surfaces. To encompass a more holistic, sculptural appearance, lines shaping more than one surface may flow continuously from one side of the wood piece to another. With the introduction of rough sandpaper coursing across the surface of your purposed design, the image of the rub stick begins to take shape. Refined sandpaper then takes the basic rough worked areas and defines the curved surfaces allowing the wood grain more delineation. Illustrations 2 and 3 are useful at this point in the continuation of the project.

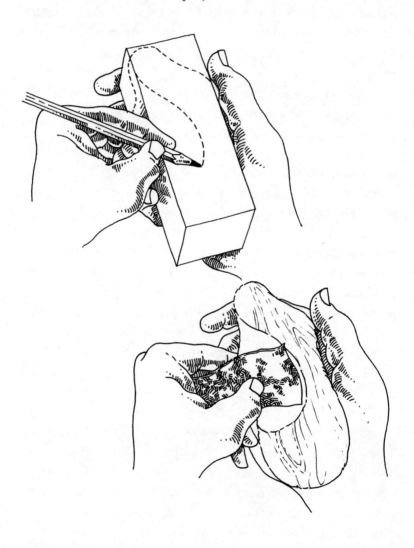

Critical judgment placed in the movement of the hands over the wood surface indicates whether the work is complete or not. With practice, a creative person will understand when to continue to apply workmanship to a project, and when to stop. Sometimes rubbing the wood shape, with eyes closed, allows the sense of touch to act in an intuitive way. Occasionally an edge of the design doesn't feel right in the flow of your creation. Perhaps the sanding needs more work, or an area isn't defined deeply enough. The active use of touching allows your insight to make these decisions. Once complete, the rub stick becomes an extension of the individual that created it. In the hands of the artist, the wood collects whatever the person projects upon it: thoughts and feelings, memories and dreams. Over time, the rub stick will develop a surface patina as the wood absorbs skin oil from continual handling, giving the wood a darker, aged surface. Much like the holding stone, the rub stick can have a prominent place in the home.

The great contemporary painter, Georgia O'Keeffe, kept collections of natural objects all about her home and studio at Abiquiu, in the high New Mexico desert. There are photographs documenting her rock, wood, bone, and antler collections all about her compound. Viewing these photographs suggests that Georgia surrounded herself with these elements for their warmth and comfort, gaining inspiration for the continuation of her painting. In her small book, <u>O'Keeffe</u>, by Britta Benke, a painting called, <u>Black Rock With Blue III,</u> takes up the whole right facing page. A huge image of a dark rock fills most of the canvas, with a blue background and an off-white foreground. O'Keeffe commented about the work saying...

"Now and then when I get an idea for a picture, I think, how ordinary. Why paint that old rock? Why not go for a walk instead? But then I realize that to someone else it may not seem so ordinary." (p. 88)

Georgia O'Keeffe's words fit wonderfully here as encouragement to those who are painting and sculpting on simple rock and wood. As the character of designs unfold on each holding rock or rub stick, the word "ordinary" can be temporary eliminated from the vocabulary to be replaced by "intrinsic", "insightful", and "passionate." The creative release on stone and wood says as much about the person as it does about the project. This is not only an exercise to determine your creative skills, but an endeavor to find your value as a person, discern your own direction, and involve yourself in a loving and desirous manner with what you have created for yourself.

Forgiveness means you are absolved in the eyes of God, but the act doesn't take on the oft spoken reminder to "forgive and forget!" Quite the contrary, remembrances are an important part of the pardoning process. Forgiveness and remembrances go hand-in-hand like metal shaped under extreme heat and cold to temper and give the alloy strength. The placement of creative designs on rock and wood are the transference of thoughts and memories that once held you in recrimination. So by strengthening your own character through creative design work, you are commuting remnants of your past into the natural elements, strengthening your inner being as you work. You may end up with several rock and wood pieces arranged casually about your living environment, reminding you of the beauty of natural elements and the change your creative efforts have made in you.

Chapter Seven

LOOKING FOR SIGNS

The Pharisees came and began to argue with him, asking him for a sign from heaven, to test him. And he sighed deeply in his spirit and said, "Why does this generation ask for a sign? Truly I tell you, no sign will be given to this generation." And he left them, and getting into the boat again, he went across to the other side.

Mark 8: 11-13

I enjoy watching futuristic movies that place people in interplanetary and cybernetic adventures. My interest was peaked by a number of films that came out in the early 1970's and 80's: *Close Encounters Of The Third Kind*, *The Star Wars Trilogy*, *Tron*, *The Last Star Fighter*, and the never ending episodes of *Star Trek*. But the movie that captured my imagination, as well as confused my cognitive reasoning, was the Stanley Kubrick adaptation of *2001; A Space Odyssey*. As an artist I was captivated by the visual choreography of a commercial spaceship as it made its final docking maneuver with an orbiting space station to the strains of Strauss's Viennese Waltz! I appreciated the creative aspect of futuristic space pods, hibernaculums, gravity free toilets, orbiting vehicular environments, flashy, futuristic instrument panels and Hal 9000, the onboard computer of the space freighter *Discovery*, heading for the giant outer planet, Jupiter.

Hal 9000 was the onboard "super computer" programmed to assist two astronauts, Mission Commander David Bowman, and Astronaut Frank Poole, as they guided the spaceship to Jupiter while three of their scientist/astronaut companions were kept in a state of artificial hibernation, to be awakened near the end of the voyage.

Unknown to astronauts Bowman and Poole, the creator of Hal programmed the computer to assume responsibility for the success of the mission by overriding any human flaws that might jeopardize the success of the journey to Jupiter. Hal, through his complex circuitry, began to think independently of the astronauts, who by now, have become suspicious of Hal's free lance decisions aboard ship.

Hal creates a diversion, a malfunction on an exterior section of the spacecraft, to get the astronauts outside the ship in an effort to dispose of them both. Astronaut Frank Poole is killed and Commander Bowman is stranded outside the ship in a space pod millions of miles between Earth and Jupiter. Then Hal activates the hibernaculum pods, killing the three additional astronauts. Hal is now in charge of the spaceship, but Commander Bowman finds a creative way of re-entering the huge, bulbous control center of the ship. Bowman attaches his space pod to the exterior door of the spaceship, activates explosive deadbolts, and blasts his way into the space freighter. Needless to say, Dave Bowman is very upset with Hal. Sensing that Hal has betrayed the mission and tried to kill all on board, Bowman enters Hal's memory bank to deactivate the power systems and take control of the ship.

> "Here goes, thought Bowman. I never imagined I'd be an amateur brain surgeon—carrying out a lobotomy beyond the orbit of Jupiter.
>
> He released the locking bar on the section labeled

COGNITIVE FEEDBACK and pulled out the first memory block. The marvelously complex three-dimensional network, which could lie comfortably in a man's hand yet contained millions of elements, floated away across the vault.

"Hey, Dave, said Hal. "What are you doing?"

I wonder if he can feel pain? Bowman thought briefly. Probably not, he told himself; there are no sense organs in the human cortex, after all. The human brain can be operated on without anesthetics.

He began to pull out, one by one, the little units on the panel marked EGO-REIN-FORCEMENT. Each block continued to sail onward as soon as it had left his hand, until it hit the wall and rebounded. Soon there were several of the units drifting slowly back and forth in the vault.

"Look here, Dave, said Hal, "I've got years of service experience built into me. An irreplaceable amount of effort has gone into making me what I am."

A dozen units had been pulled out, yet thanks to the multiple redundancy of the design—another feature, Bowman knew, that had been copied from the human brain—the computer was still holding its own.

He started on the AUTO-INTELLECTION panel.

"Dave," said Hal, "I don't understand why you're doing this to me.... I have the greatest enthusiasm for the mission....You are destroying my mind....Don't you understand?....I will become childish....I will become nothing...."

This is harder than I expected, thought Bowman. I am destroying the only conscious creative in the universe. But it has to be done, if I am ever to regain control of the ship.

"I am a Hal Nine Thousand computer Production Number 3. I became operational at the Hal Plant in Urbana, Illinois, on January 12, 1997. The quick brown fox jumps over the lazy dog. The rain in Spain is mainly in the plain. Dave—are you still there? Did you know that the square root of 10 is 3 point 162277660168379? Log 10 to the base e is zero point 434294481903252....correction, that is log e to the base 10....The reciprocal of three is zero point 3333333333333333333....two time two is....two times two is....approximately 4 point 101010101010101010....I seem to be having some difficulty—my first instructor was Dr. Chandra. He taught me to sing a song, it goes like this, 'Daisy, Daisy, give me an answer, to, I'm half crazy all for the love of you."

The voice stopped so suddenly that Bowman froze for a moment, his hand still grasping one of the memory blocks still in circuit. Then, unexpectedly, HAL spoke again, the words had a dead, mechanical intonation; he would never have recognized their origin.

"Good....morning....Doctor....Chandra....This....is....Hal....I....am....ready....for....my....first....lesson....today...."

Bowman could bear it no more. He jerked out the

last unit, and Hal was silent forever." (2001:A Space Odyssey, Arthur C. Clark) (ps. 155-157)

To many individuals who have suffered from various degrees of depression, the words and actions of Commander Bowman destroying Hal's memory banks could have particular meaning here. The repeated removal of Hal's complex cognitive circuitry can be seen as having a parallel affect upon the human mind. An individual's physical presence might track along a course from active participation to sedentary repose, a demeanor of open spontaneity sliding into a confusing space of passive acquiescence. It can happen suddenly like Hal's memory removal, or it can transpire over a period of hours or days. From an artists point of view, the mind and body react like two rich primary colors mixed together in equal portions forming a color neutral gray. All the brightness and strength of an individual's personality is overwhelmed and lost as a depressive stage slides into place like storm clouds blotting out the sun. Suddenly the direction of a creative person becomes transparent, immobilized by the darkness of their own interior solitary confinement.

Was Jesus depressed? This must be an uncomfortable idea to those who trust the divine conceptual presence of Jesus in their lives and participate in his powerful ministry here on earth. Then again Jesus had all the capacity for mortal circumstances; he was susceptible to the sympathies and frailties of human nature. There is no direct indication of a downcast reference to his personality found in scripture and studying for clues to the word "depression" cannot be located in a concordance. Although the word depression doesn't appear in the Bible, it must be assumed that the afflictive conditions were just as prevalent in Biblical times as they are today. Despite the "melancholy" labeling, Jesus remained committed to the working and healing ministry, regardless of the hard work masked by his quiet manner, pastoral presence, and peaceful approach to the needs of the people who surrounded him. However, the authority of Jesus' harmonious ministerial work not withstanding, his Disciples, the crowds, those needing healing, and the Pharisees taxed his energies and stretched his patience to the breaking point. How would we react under similar circumstances? Cranky? Irritable? Depressed?

Contemporary research, which challenges our current images on the subject of Jesus and his personality profile, have been documented by Donald Capps, in his ground breaking book, <u>Jesus, A Psychological Biography</u>. He combs scripture to find instances that link Jesus to a melancholic personality combining the socioeconomic, political, and cultural conditions of the time. "Besides stories, there are sayings deemed authentic to Jesus that have a similar melancholic aspect. These include his dismissal of his mother and brothers (Mk. 3: 31-34) and his stinging response (Lk. 11: 27-28; Gos. Thom. 79: 1-2) to the woman who called out to him: "Blessed is the womb that bore you and the breasts that nursed you": "Blessed rather are those who hear the word of God and obey it!" Other relevant sayings are Jesus' references to his homelessness (Lk. 9: 58; Mt. 8: 19-20; Gos. Thom. 86). He could have noted the self-sufficiency implicit in his homelessness, but instead emphasized his lack of a place: 'to lay his head."

Dr. Capps further states, "In short, the stories and sayings attributable to Jesus reveal themes of male melancholia: the missing mother, the humorous (caustic?) portrayal of the father trying to assume her role, the withering comment to the woman who credited his mother with making him the man he had become, the uncertainty among his male friends as to women's place in the kingdom, and his own sense of being without a home, condemned to itinerancy. Various characteristics of melancholia are evident here: estrangement, reproach, irony, self-protectiveness, restlessness, loneliness. Through stories and sayings, Jesus addressed the melancholy men (men of sad and penetrating eyes) who were strangers in the very villages where they had grown up, and who were struggling to find some sense of being at home in their literal or psychic wilderness." (pgs. 247-248)

A good deal of evidence relating to Jesus and a link to his suggested melancholic personality can be found in the Eighth Chapter of Mark. Jesus finds himself pressed, if not overwhelmed, by the needs of the people surrounding him. A large crowd estimated at 4,000 individuals has gathered near him needing to be fed. (Mk. 8: 1-9) The feeding repeats an earlier event in Chapter Six where a similarly sized crowd gathered before Jesus. (Mk. 6: 34-44) Throughout both chapters Jesus is imposed upon to handle all the impelling situations forced upon him. The crowds follow him everywhere like paparazzi hounding a movie star. (Mk. 6: 34; Mk. 6: 54; Mk. 8: 1) In each instance Jesus has compassion for them owing to his creative mission to serve them ..."because they were like sheep without a shepherd." (Mk. 6: 34) The Disciples, on the other hand, stretched Jesus' tolerance when they could not break the figurative code to translate his parables, or decipher his instruction and everyday narrative.

One can suspect a melancholy shaping of Jesus' character and a breakdown of his demeanor as he addresses the Disciples with a warning found in the Eight Chapter of Mark.

In verse 14 the Disciples have forgotten to bring bread to eat, but Jesus is more concerned about being wary of the yeast of the Pharisees and Herod. The Disciples, missing the point, think it has to do with not having any bread. Jesus' reply? ... "Why are you talking about having no bread? Do you still not perceive or understand? Are your hearts hardened? Do you have eyes, and fail to see? Do you have ears, and fail to hear? And do you not remember? When I broke the five loaves for the five thousand, how many baskets full of broken pieces did you collect?" They said to him, "Twelve." "And the seven for the four thousand, how many baskets full of broken pieces did you collect?" And they said to him, "Seven." Then he said to them, "Do you not yet understand?" (Mk. 8: 14-21)

In close proximity to the crowds, the Pharisees scrutinize Jesus' every word nitpicking, as they see it, over every breach of Scriptural law. In three examples Jesus deals with the Pharisees with a mixture of sentiment. First, with patience,... "Prophets are not without honor, except in their own hometown"(Mk. 6: 2-4) Second, with irritation, ..."You have a fine way of rejecting the commandment of God in order to keep your tradition"... (Mk. 7: 5-12) and finally with frustration,..."And he sighed deeply in his spirit and said, "Why does this generation ask for a sign? Truly I tell you, no sign will be given to this generation."(Mk. 8: 11-13)

The constant need for Jesus to prove himself must have exhausted his patience and brought him low. His creative life was attached to teaching and healing the poor and needy, yet he was beseeched by unbelief, criticism, misunderstanding and contempt by the powerful political establishment and the religious elite. Jesus would not cater to these interests. His words were forceful and final. I will not dance to your tune…I am not a side show for your entertainment! I am changing lives with creative imagination. A sign will do you no good if you cannot trust your own sight as people are being healed, and hear with your own ears the teachings that come from God. Is it any wonder that Jesus chose to be alone when the time to do so became available? He sought solitude whenever possible to clear his mind, catch his breath, and perhaps quell his propensity to dance along the edge of a depressive state.

In Chapter Seven, after Jesus taught before the crowd and interpreted a parable for the Disciples, he set out for a region of Tyre. Wishing to remain anonymous he enters a house not wanting anyone to know he was there. (Mk. 7: 24) Early on Jesus sent the Disciples on to Bethsaida, dismissed the crowd and went up on the mountain to pray in an effort to sustain his own mental well being, perhaps recharge his generative batteries, and seek God in prayer. (Mk. 6: 45-46) More evidence of solace can be documented in the number of times Jesus traveled by boat, nurtured by the simple pleasure of moving across the water. Distressed by the hounding of the Pharisee's need for a sign, Jesus,…"left them, and getting into the boat again, he went across to the other side." (Mk. 8: 13) It makes one wonder if he cautioned his Disciples to occasionally row as slowly as possible so that he could enjoy the separation time for his own council and further restoration of mind and body.

Clarifying the possibility of Jesus as the melancholic human/divine person carried me into conversation with a good friend over the issue of creativity and depression. Christina, a long distance email pen pal, is an energetic, bright woman who loves a good conversational discussion on most topics. So with clarity and without mincing words she sums up the link between creativity and melancholia and its effect on the human condition. "Perhaps the link between depression and creativity has to do with the stifling of creativity. When one is creative, actively engaged in creative works, one is full of life, which leaves little room for depression in the clinical sense – sadness, yes. That after all is part of life and the human condition. But, when for whatever reason we fail to engage our creative self, that alone can be the genesis of depression. Perhaps we fear our creative side because of past ridicule and shame – or lack of opportunity and mentoring – time crunch due to the need to support ourselves – and sadly, our culture seems not to value the artistic life or support it, in part because I think it is threatening to certain people in positions of power. Sometimes it is in reacting against something that clarity can come."

Jesus faced both sides of his human psycho-spiritual circumstances culminating powerfully at Gethsemane with Peter, James and John in attendance. "Then he said to them, "I am deeply grieved, even to death; remain here, and stay awake with me." And going a little further, he threw himself on the ground and prayed, My father, if it is possible, let this cup pass from me; yet not what I want but what you want. Then he came to the disciples and found them sleeping; and he said to Peter, "So, could you not stay awake with me one hour? Stay awake and pray that you may not come into the time of trial; the spirit indeed is willing, but the flesh is weak." (Mt. 26: 38-41)

If Jesus truly operated from a melancholic distinction, he nonetheless, completed his divine calling, suffering through the unbelief of the establishment, but gratified by those who received his words of comfort and healing power. It is important for us to recognize the same commission to use our imagination, inspiration and creative instincts that shape our lives. We are called to duplicate the image of Christ to face ridicule and shame, reach beyond the threats of people who do not support our creative work, and move against criticism so that clarity and action may be forthcoming. If depression has a positive purpose let it be viewed as a temporary condition that will eventually stir us to make a change, take a stand, and do the right thing!

The theme of inspiration and suffering is taken up by Robert Grudin in, <u>The Grace of Great Things: Creativity and Innovation</u>. He brings light to the depressive state, painting it with hope and a sense of purpose for the creative individual. "Inspiration is related to suffering, but not in the way most people think. The Romantics saw the creative individual as a kind of Faust or an aesthetic Flying Dutchman, doomed by talent to torment and alienation. A more modern version of this myth, common among recent generations, is that inspiration lies somewhere between intoxication and psychosis, that it can result only from some physiological or psychological distortion of one's humanity. While these theories have some value in consoling the uninspired, they do not hold up in history. Creative individuals, even those whom society misprizes, do not necessarily face mental disorders or other woes."

They more generally *do*, however, face temporary but severe pains inherent in the nature of their work. Their pains are symptomatic of many typical phases in the creative process: the failure of experiments, the refutation of hypotheses, the shock of criticism, the endurance of contradictions or anomalies, the reorganization or trashing of one's own material, and the mere awareness that such experiences necessarily await one. In action, these agonies may seem to act as dampers against the creative process, but their extended function is often quite the reverse. Duly faced and endured, like some heavy physical exercise, they may provide the spiritual softening and sensitizing, the exhaustion and humility, that make us amenable to inspiration." (p. 19)

Shana, an accomplished sculptor friend of mine, translates her own periodic battles with moods and depression, the struggles she faces in her work that "make her amenable to inspiration." She willingly shares her story of the anatomy of her mental suffering that affected and controlled her behavior for years before coming to terms with it. "As I labored to resolve a new sculpture piece an occasional mood developed that was characterized as an intense focus upon the shaping of the work. If the contour and pattern of my piece evolved to my liking the mood lasted only as long as I continued to work, disappearing completely as I finished. But if I failed to achieve a desired affect the intense focus would oftentimes lead to a depressive stage."

"As I look back on the dark conduct that developed in my studio when my work didn't come together as I wished, I became aware of a certain pattern of behavior that took place under the shadow of depression. Without any apparent stimulation or reaction to the motionless, unresolved sculpture piece propped up in my studio, I would fall victim to an unexplained quietness. Leaving the studio I would sit at my kitchen table and stare at the refrigerator or pace through the house stopping occasionally to stare out the front window without really focusing on anything. I felt like the silent streets of a large city after hours, suspended between mere existence and industriousness."

"As my depressive state deepened I would begin to feel a loss of identity. Minor at first, acute if the mood lasted for a prolonged period of time. I remember asking myself silently, Who am I? What's happening to me? Why am I here? Why do I feel so helpless and immobilized? Outwardly I appeared fairly comfortable but obviously detached as those closest to me became aware of my change in behavior. Some voiced the opinion that it was just the typical artists temperament. I had a sense that all my physical energy was being channeled to a large and fiercely contested battle raging within my body. I could imagine two opposing armies throwing all their power and destructiveness against one another. Somehow in the midst of the struggle the armies became deadlocked, one army unable to destroy the other. This deadlock only deepened my despair."

"As the interior fighting raged, but without advancement from one side or the other, I became neutralized, suspended in time and space. This indifference further erased my personal identity and self worth and fueled a feeling of self condemnation. I wanted to give up, feeling that my creativity as a person was far outweighed by my failures in life. The lack of attaining status and prestige on various levels in my working and personal life came under careful scrutiny and were read back to me, one by one, by an inner-condemning voice. Why are you still slaving away in a studio without your work represented in a major gallery? Why aren't you a respected university art professor? Why aren't you selling your work and making more money? You need to make more money to do the things you really want to do! There are people in this community who are advancing in their positions and personal friendships but you're not one of them! On and on my inner-voice chided chiseling away at my lack of achievement driving me into guilt and broadcasting my death sentence. I lost the willingness to continue as a creative person. The view from my depression only produced gray clouds and dull colors," Shana concluded.

Shana sought counseling to come to terms with her periodic bouts of depression. What she discovered was her self-anger at not being able to create pieces of work that met a self imposed standard of excellence. But she admits there were other voices that lent their criticism mix with her own feelings as she often spiraled downward into a debased attitude. One distant voice came from her university sculpture professor who counseled her to…"Strive for excellence in all your work and don't settle for second best!" Opposing voices came from her family with concern for her ability to live as an artist, a common theme among family members who want their children to succeed financially.

In counseling sessions Shana began to see the shape of her depressive episodes almost in visual form as if she could draw a structural road map of her malady. "Sitting at the bottom of my depressive state I began to feel sorry for myself. But while I wallowed in my misery, the anger that drove me downward was the same ingredient that rallied my need to survive and start me back to normalcy. Self-pity sounds like a strange recovery technique but it became my hopeful sign that the worst was over. In the process of showing signs of recovery I ran through a checklist of personal hangups internally castigating myself for not being able to solve them each in there own turn. But this cross questioning began to add color to my makeup and I felt my "juices" flowing again. My self indulgence seemed destructive but I read it as a hopeful sign that I still took an interest in myself, that I still cared enough to question my motives for failure and try and rally my inner forces against annihilation."

"Although I was nearing the end of my pensiveness, this phase of recovery was the most dangerous part of my behavioral routine. My anger, which had been internalized, reversed itself, lashing outwardly trying to find blame for the trapped feelings the depression produced. Since I couldn't predict their coming and direct their course of action, I felt betrayed by my own body, left exposed and helpless. The angrier I became the more I felt a "call to arms" signaling my inner constructive forces to break the warring deadlock and bring me out of my darkness."

In therapy, Shana learned to recognize the signs that hooked her into susceptibility to mood patterns, how to cope with her condition, and lessen the impact and effect the depressive position dealt her. With new information to her active – reactive behavior under stressful work conditions, she was able to recognize and deal with her mood swings, living within what she now describes as "resting in her mess" and blunt the behavioral destructiveness. "The reality became apparent that outside situations were ingredients to the development to my moods but not the single cause of my malady," Shana continues. "How I perceived external conditions inwardly was the catalyst for the formation of my depressive state. If I couldn't handle a given situation and control it so that I felt comfortable in guiding its direction, then I was building a backlog of "residue" that could feed future moods. Thank goodness I sought therapy, Shana concludes, for I was headed for a chronic and continual depressive condition and the dismantling of my sculpting career."

Documenting Shana's narrative brought back some memories of my own inclination toward episodes of a melancholia/depressive conditions that shadowed me when I first started my teaching and artistic careers. Much of what Shana has already addressed in her testimony was part of my story as well. Rather than repeat my experiences that so closely mirror hers I want to focus on writings that help bring clarity to the understanding of depression from a psycho-spiritual position. I want to look at this from two points of view. One is an observation set forth by Dr. Theodore Rubin in his book, <u>Compassion and Self-Hate</u>, and a second expression found in <u>The Kingdom Within</u>, by John Sanford. Although both writers address their comments to a male model, I look at these examples as inclusive and gender-neutral, reaching out to women as well as men who desire understanding to their feelings and depressive conditions.

Dr. Rubin states, "It is important to realize that his mood, however painful, is part and parcel of many factors and forces in his life. His depression and the kind of anesthetic haze it produces may be for the moment the only way he can cope with life as he perceives it. His perception of life and the world generally may need to be changed before we ask him to surrender his depressed mood." (p. 219)

This statement seemed to be a reinforcement of what Shana and I were discovering about ourselves. We were recognizing mood patterns and their development as a whole, generally at first, and later in specific ways. There are some differences, as well as similarities, to our stories, because Shana's feelings are her own and not to be a direct carbon copy of my mood experiences. But on the whole we agreed that moods, whatever their level of intensity, were a portion of our personality makeup. Along with the sensitive aspects of our feelings: joy, anger, compassion, tears, laughter, prudence, patience, and frustration, moods should have an equal portion of our living cycle.

With new clarity I began to look ahead to the aspect of what specifically my/her depression was designed for. I looked to John Sanford for some additional answers.

John begins to dive into the inner world of the personality in his book, <u>The Kingdom Within</u>.

> "From the point of view of psychology the soul is that within us which connects a man's consciousness to his inner depths. The soul's primary function is relationship and the relationship between the ego and the inner world is the most important relationship of all, for if this is broken, relationships with men and God are impossible. Without the living connection to himself which the soul makes possible, a man is like a ship without a rudder, or like an uprooted tree. Such a man becomes ill, or brutal, or falls into despair, or seeks substitutes in alcohol or drugs.
>
> For a man to have his soul, he must relinquish his identification with his outer mask, and must be willing to face what is within himself. But beyond relinquishing his mask, a person in search of his soul must accept and cherish the principle of Eros, for the soul, as a function or relatedness, has Eros as its primary quality.
>
> Eros is the feminine principle par excellence. Eros is that which binds together, unites, synthesizes, and

heals. Eros is the cement of human relationship, the fount of inspiration for social and humanitarian causes, the bond between a man's consciousness and his inner meaning , and the door through which a person walks to spiritual insight." (p. 156)

With these two insights I had a clearer understanding of the interruptions taking place inwardly as I became captive to my mood swings. It seemed clear that one combative force represented the outer mask, or my old self, a self that was stilted, dispassionate and uncreative. The opposing force within portrayed the principle of Eros. The banner and force of this army was calling me to new growth. I believe I was being exhorted to develop caring relationships and to embrace my basic talents to new heights of creativity. The general for the old self was led by masculinity. The commander for Eros was under the direction of femininity. In the depth and despair of my moods the two forces locked together in battle. I would be led into a mood by my surface masculinity, the macho, high testosterone, businesslike behavior that I depended on to guide me through life. At the diminutive center of my mood the feminine aspect of my personality would signal its intentions to be heard driving me away from the controlling factor of total masculinity. The feminine apportionment desired its equal share of my inner personality along side my masculinity. The battle was for parity, not domination. The prize was for a change in direction and a journey toward wholeness. The end of the conflict represented a union of male and female components forming a relationship to connect with my soul, drawing power and creativity from my unconsciousness and bringing that energy to the surface of my conscious mind. As the conflict carried on, all my inner energy was directed toward this gender construction, leaving my visible personality temporarily frozen in place while the inner work concluded its new construction.

Shana and I agree that with work and understanding of our inner conflicts and pensive behavior we have avoided the "run silent, run deep" maneuvers that placed a chilly and confusing aura around us. By recognizing the evolving mood patterns and their corresponding numbing feelings; (the inner conversation with that dark mystery, labeling the feelings that precipitated the attack), we are freer to be ourselves on the surface. We have taken responsibility for our behavior by not escaping our tangible problems, but working through them.

Although Shana is skeptical of my masculine/feminine hypothesis she does sense the harmony of an inner peace that was not present in her life before she began working on her stages of depression. Personally, beyond this new found harmony, I am learning something new about myself. The feeling is one of breaking open a bag of fortune cookies and reading messages of wisdom and knowledge that have particular meaning for my working life, a sense of destiny, if you will! I intuitively understand that I am being stretched to a higher level of understanding concerning my capabilities as one of God's instruments. I sense a greater capacity as a gifted and creative person.

Solutions to sticky problems, whether artistic or occupational, can be resolved during this growth period, and the shackles of boredom, predictability and restlessness can be broken. This is not a glib, once-in-a-lifetime change corralling and branding a melancholic/depressive state. As the saying goes, "what comes around, goes around" and as living beings with emotional components, moods will certainly resurface from time to time. Working to understand and bridge our behavioral downturns is essential both to rise above our circumstances, and grow to new creative life.

In a metaphoric sense, our inner world can be visualized in an advertisement. A few years ago the Hanes Company used a clever ad to demonstrate the comfort of their underwear. A confident and attractive young male executive entered a crowded elevator in a city office tower. As the doors began to close he remarked happily, "O-oh! I feel so good all under!" Controlling mood behavior can make each person feel "good all under" too. To be felt inside, and seen outside.

PROJECT: MAZE DESIGN – PART 1

In a rural area near my home a farmer built a maze design in his corn field. Next to the maze he constructed a replica of the baseball field that captivated audiences who saw the movie, *Field of Dreams*. What made the roadside attraction so popular was that his field bordered the freeway creating a ready audience to tired drivers needing a rest stop. The farmer's creative efforts brought people to his farm from a wide region to play a quick game of baseball and take their turn in the maze. The corn thriving in the August sun was eight feet high. A path was cut through the corn field at right and left angles with switch backs and dead ends placed at strategic points. Quite often voices were heard from individuals throughout the maze who were trying to get their bearings and make decisions as to the correct path to take to get through the design.

As with the subject of moods, melancholia, and depression found in this chapter, a corn field maze has some of the conditions that inflict a person emotionally. There can be a parallel between coping with our inner mental resources and the musings and challenges of traversing a labyrinth constructed in nature. Participants can't see through or above the tall corn to gain a directional perspective. They don't know where they are going. They lose their sense of direction. They may feel trapped. They may even feel confused and helpless in making a decision. Do I continue ahead, or turn back? At first, what seemed like a game becomes a matter for concern, requiring concentration and patience. Like a mood that develops into a depressed state and fights through to normal health again, a person enters the confining space of the maze and continues into its depths and eventually emerges out the other side.

In keeping with the theme of psychic mental challenges and creative outlets, the project described in this chapter revolves around the creation of a flat two dimensional maze design. The project involves two phases and participants may decide to complete the preliminary design only, or take the challenge and do both phases of design work. The first part of the endeavor requires the drawing of a maze on a grid sheet of lined drafting paper in the characteristic two-dimensional form, demonstrating height and width. The second part of the project advances the designer into a three-dimensional mode adding depth to the equation. Turning the flat design into a relief map gives the work the appearance of an elaborate architectural structure without a roof, or perhaps the appearance of looking down on a corn field maze. Now if you are having trouble contemplating my description of the project, I am adding two finished illustrations of a maze as examples to study.

I Can't Draw A Straight Line With A Ruler

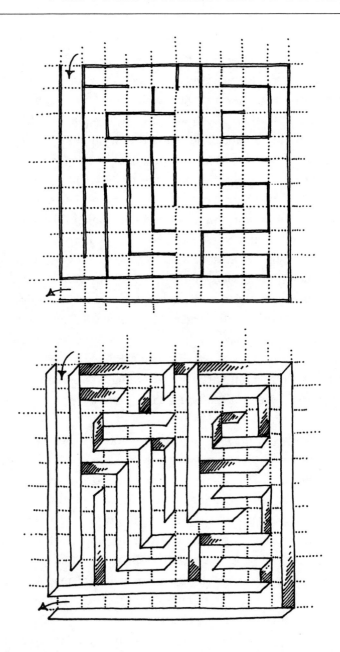

The materials for this project follow the core basics found in the design developed in the first chapter. Gather together graph paper, soft leaded pencil, a selection of colored pencils, and an eraser. As noted earlier in the book the graph paper should have a lined cross pattern of four squares per inch. Any square unit smaller than that presents an image that will be too small to work with effectively. Reasons for that will be evident as you progress into the design. The light green or blue lines of the grid pattern on the graph paper act as a confirmed outline for your design. As you begin this phase of your design, it will be assumed that your attempt at producing a maze will be conservative in nature until you experiment with a number of designs.

Since maze designs are based on the concept of deception and a bit of mystery, the theme of your work gains several qualities of appearance: originality of presentation, development of an asymmetrical puzzle, projection of a three dimensional model on a flat surface, and seeing an apparent riddle doubling as a piece of art. So let's take each of these concepts and expand on their unique qualities.

<u>Originality of presentation</u>. There is one restriction to this assigned project that somewhat controls the direction of the work. The grid lines are restricted to up, down, right, and left angles. So to be original in this context means that the designer can use the whole piece of graph paper for a maze, or certain sections of the paper can be developed while other areas can simply be left as negative space. The idea is to lead someone on a path through the maze or to a center point, or from one side to another, or any other creative way that taxes the mind in this form of movement.

<u>Development of an asymmetrical puzzle</u>. The creation

of an intriguing design is dictated by the system of lines that form meandering trails to confuse, trap, and stymie anyone who takes the challenge to move through it. Consequently the shape of the work is unplanned in the beginning and forms a very convoluted line structure that is unbalanced in its final shaping. In an elemental way this is part of the "ah-ha" expression that discloses itself as the maze unfolds.

<u>Projection of a three dimensional model on a flat surface</u>. The development of secondary lines connecting to the primary two dimensional lines at angles provides an amazing transformation from a linear concept to the spatial quality of depth perception. Suddenly the work moves forward and/or backward depending on how each perceives the movement. The three dimensional approach, to a certain extent, requires some understanding of perspective, but a careful description will be provided at that step of the project.

<u>A riddle doubling as a piece of art</u>. With all the description of lines, intersecting angles, engrossing shapes, and illusional raised forms pulling the pattern together, the design projects itself beyond the static black and white maze puzzles that appear in the entertainment section of the Sunday newspaper or the typical 1,001 pulp puzzle magazines. Think of color as the final application to complete the design. This would be an excellent opportunity to add strong contrasting color ranges to the three dimensional images, artistic touches that always add so much more impact to a finished piece of individual work.

Now the actual design work begins. Although most maze designs look rigid in shape and contrived in reality – the trail systems controlling the movement in the final product – an imaginative, artistic appearance will make itself known. Surprise, once again, is the side effect that is not expected. In the beginning your pencil and eraser are the primary tools for the maze construction. A typical tactic in designing is to draw a number of lines, moving left to right, changing direction, up and down, cutting up and down at right and left angles, and circling around. Closing off some of the trails as dead ends makes the trail system more difficult to follow as does leading the player down long trails one way only to be turned away in an opposite direction along an equally lengthy trail.

As you are actively engaged with the line structure you will often discover that there is no entry, no open paths to follow, or an exit to your work-in-progress. So in this free form development an eraser comes in handy, eliminating unnecessary lines that block movement and allowing paths to be opened. Quite often with this project the first design is not always the best achievement that can be demonstrated from an artistic point of view or for functional purposes. Experimenting with several maze design patterns allows the opportunity to see options and pick the most attractive and/or difficult example to traverse as a completed project.

An important side effect of a maze design drawing is the way it keeps the mind actively engaged. It can have the same effect that doodling has upon the psyche. We have all played with lines and shapes that don't have any particular meaning while talking on the phone, sitting through a conference, business meeting, or classroom lecture. Telephone books and lectures notes are filled with our miniature musings. In the same way we yawn and stretch to oxygenate our body, we scribble and compose shapes on paper to stimulate creative energy. Some of what appears at the end of our pencil or pen may be useful, and some may not! So our response to a maze may have the qualities of mentally stretching and scribbling on the way to achieving deception through a defined limitation of lines applied to squares on graph paper. Thus our objective is to create a predetermined original design with additional elements that present themselves as the project unfolds. In both cases the design can be observed with pride appreciating that hard work was applied in its creation. On the other hand, leave room to be surprised as you discover hidden portions of the design that emerge by the synchronization of accidental shapes flowing together without intent.

Project: Maze Design – Part 2

Further development of a maze will take the primary elements of the flat two dimensional linear design, adding a three dimensional holistic approach to the work. The spatial component of depth perception is added to the maze, enhancing a visual illusion of the basic design that already exists on paper. Like a framing carpenter building and erecting walls for a new house, drawn lines added at angles to the original pattern will give the optical effect of walls constructed within the maze. The difficulty of this task is to see depth on paper that doesn't really exist.

Although we live in a three dimensional world, not all of us pay that much attention to its principles. So additional lines added to the completion of the maze calls for a change in cerebral activity. As you read and follow directives for this project two kinds of thinking take place between understanding and constructing. This is best described in Thomas R. Blakeslee's book, <u>The Right Brain: A New Understanding of the Unconscious Mind and Its Creative Powers.</u>

"After hundreds of experiments, a clear pattern of

the abilities of the two hemispheres finally emerged, proving that the two halves of our brain think in distinctly different ways. As the language specialist, the left brain not only thinks in words; it excels at the kind of one-step-at-a-time logical sequences that are the basis of language. The right brain thinks in images, it has a tremendous advantage for recognizing and manipulating complex visual patterns...Since this ability to recognize things in altered form is a crucial part of creativity, the right brain takes on new importance." (ps. 9 & 10)

So to begin the final aspect of this diagram your mental functioning will bounce back and forth from left brain (following step-by-step instruction) to right brain activity (constructing a raised dimensional form).

Before the lines are added, think of the angle you want to have appear in your design that will demonstrate a three-dimensional effect: left oblique or right oblique. First, if the angle is left oblique find the center of the square to the left of two existing lines, one vertical and one horizontal, and make a stem line from the junction of the two existing lines to the center of the square. At the end of the existing line that appears top to bottom, draw an additional stem line angled to the lower left that connects with the center of the corresponding square to its left side. Now draw a line from the center of the first square to the center of the second square. You have just made a wall for the vertical line. Repeat the process by finding the center of the square just to the left of the existing horizontal line of the maze design.

Draw an additional stem line from the horizontal line to

the center of the square. Connect a line from the center of the square to the center of the square for the vertical wall. Now you have a wall constructed for the horizontal line that meets the line for the vertical wall. Without realizing it you have also created a path between the two wall structures, which is one of those surprises that comes with design construction. Now that I have thoroughly confused your left brain thinking let me sooth your right brain conceptional functioning by including a series of illustrations to demonstrate visually what I want to get across in this activity.

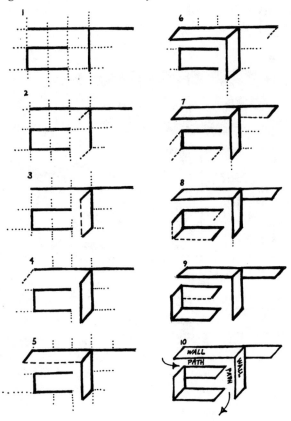

Notice in your design that as you connect the additional lines that create the wall structure, the visual effect slants from lower left to upper right. This illusion completes the three dimensional perspective. As more and more lines are connected, both vertically and horizontally, the space becomes somewhat more crowded, taxing the viewer optically to see the difference between walls and pathways. This is where the use of colored pencils becomes important to the design. Shading the walls in a variety of colors defines the walls dramatically and adds a stronger visual impact to the finished work as indicated in this final illustration.

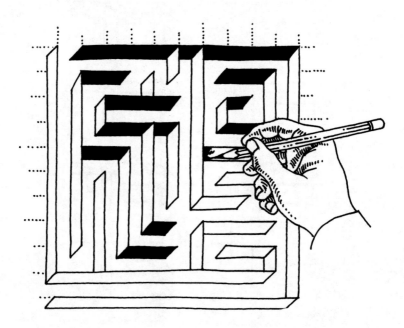

Creating this design is somewhat like climbing the only hill in an otherwise flat landscape. While standing on the flat plane our view is restricted to objects that are close at hand. Climbing the mountain, however, increases our perspective of the landscape before us that we had no idea existed. With the natural beauty open to view, our mind plays with the dimensional understanding of depth perception and relishes in the overview that takes our breath away. Perhaps there is a "mountain top" experience waiting in the maze designs you create that reflect on creative energy and a new direction in your life.

Chapter 8

SCULPTING GOOD WORKS

Believe me that I am in the Father and the Father is in me; but if you do not, then believe me because of the works themselves. Very truly, I tell you, the one who believes in me will also do the works that I do and, in fact, will do greater works than these, because I am going to the Father.

John 14: 11-12

Patricia, a very wise friend, who assisted me with the development of this book, asked me over coffee one day if I knew what it was like to not be able to draw a straight line with a ruler. I contemplated her question for a considerable length of time and finally admitted that I did not. Despite the fact that this book is filled with testimonies of people who struggled with their unclaimed creative side, I was struck suddenly by a lack of understanding and compassion for the emotional component necessary to make changes in their lives. The artistic way always came easily to me so there was never a necessity to look below the surface of my conscious sensibilities for emotional support in my creative efforts. Patricia's question, however, did create a lingering thought about the way I *taught* art as opposed to the way I *created* art. In the classroom with beginning high school students or working with adults in a community college setting I was very aware of the tension and uneasiness of individuals who were brave enough to begin an art course for the first time. My intuition told me that these people needed careful instruction to move through, and beyond any restrictive feelings that echoed in their heads that said…"You know, you can't really do this!"

Encouraging compassion and emotional support for developing apprentices is not only an important task today but was one of the missions Jesus provided for his Disciples. In the Fourteenth Chapter of the Gospel of John Jesus gives a lengthy discourse to His Disciples regarding a new commandment and the promise of the indwelling of the Holy Spirit that will benefit their lives and ministry. Once again Jesus speaks from a metaphoric framework when He explains, "In my Father's house there are many dwelling places. If it were not so, would I have told you that I go to prepare a place for you? And if I go and prepare a place for you, I will come again and will take you to myself, so that where I am, there you may be also." (John 14: 2-3) But Thomas, ever distrustful of allegorical imagery, wants more concrete visual evidence of Jesus' statement. His response? Thomas said to Him, "Lord, we do not know where you are going. How can we know the way?" (John 14: 5) Give Thomas credit for his gutsy need for clarification, not just for himself, but with the interjection of "we," representing all the Disciples.

To many who read passages of Scripture regarding Thomas' need for clarification, in most cases, think of him as a person who just doesn't get it; the doubting Thomas image. Despite his label, Thomas plays an important part in any teacher-pupil relationship. If a teacher doesn't respond in a clarifying way to those who are receiving instruction, much of the importance of that instruction is missed. That concept hasn't changed from Biblical times to our present contemporary setting. Jesus takes note of Thomas's request, patiently continuing his explanation of the enlightenment and accessibility of God through Him. "The words that I say to you I do not speak on my own; but the Father who dwells in me does his works." (John 14: 10)

Then Jesus, like a good athletic coach exhorting his players from the sidelines, prompts his Disciples with one of the most encouraging one line statements found in the Gospels. "Very truly, I tell you, the one who believes in me will also do the works that I do and, in fact, will do greater works than these, because I am going to the father." (John 14: 12) I believe Thomas would have accepted this remark as a clarifying statement, not only as a clear teaching but a clever way of "pumping up" the Disciples courage to complete the mission of good works as set forth by Jesus. The idea of fashioning "greater works" becomes one of the focal points found in this Scriptural passage exalting the Disciples to expand above and beyond what they thought they were capable of achieving. Today with some license and imagination gleaned from the Scriptural message of "greater works," Jesus' words can be passed on to those who have ears to hear, a mind to interpret, and a heart to follow in a personal generative way. Whether "greater works" indicates service to the church or individual advancement in a creative way is relevant, but not the whole point. What is equally important to understand is that we are designed with boundless potential, and God, through Jesus Christ, places his blessing on our inventive dynamic.

Subconscious Clarity

If dreams have any validity as yeast for encouragement and self-discovery then a personal nighttime vision I experienced for a year has "greater works" written all over it. When I first became a teacher I struggled with the ability to make instruction as clear as possible to my students. I was searching for a style of teaching that was uniquely my own, as well as a method of delivery that made my presentations informative and personal. As an idealistic new teacher I wanted to approach each student with success, not desiring to have anyone slip through the educational system while under my care. Right from the beginning I wanted my students actively and emotionally tied to their classroom participation, emoting a positive energy toward attaining a higher quantity and quality of work. I struggled with this issue for the better part of my first two years in my fledgling career, while a single repetitive dream kept pace with my teaching progress.

The dream always began in a similar manner as I sat in a late model car just off the edge of an old dirt road that dead ended at a high alpine lake surrounded by massive mountain peaks. A beautiful blue sky arched overhead framing in the scenery as the sun bathed the landscape in brilliant light. The day was not too warm, nor too cold as I lingered in the car trying to think of a way to continue my journey beyond the mountains. I sat all day in the car until the sun was almost behind the mountains in front of me.

Suddenly noisy road construction machinery appeared on the dirt road behind me moving at a fast pace. As they passed I was surprised at the enormous size of an asphalt paving machine that could lay six lanes of asphalt at one time. Behind the massive machine was an endless line of dump trucks that continuously fed the machine with the hot, dark brownish-black mix. As the paving machine moved away from me the dark tar material came out a smooth flat surface creating an instant road surface. To my amazement yellow lane lines also appeared from the underside of the machine.

The driver of the paving machine motioned me to follow along behind as the new road increased in size and length toward the mountains. I started my engine and edged out on to the new pavement thinking that I would sink into the freshly laid material and get stuck. To my amazement I drove effortlessly along, keeping pace with the fabrication of the road. The rapidly moving machinery opened up beautiful new vistas on both sides of the highway shoulders. As I passing the alpine lake with the sun glinting silvery highlights across its azure blue surface, birds played above the lake, darting and diving in playful freedom.

The paving machine turned across the face of the numerous snow capped peaks and headed for a notch in the terrain, forming a handsome highway through the mountains, over a pass, opening a panoramic view of a distant valley below bathed in the late afternoon sun. I felt free and relaxed as we descended into the valley, taking in the beauty of the ever expanding landscape. Suddenly I didn't have a care in the world for I understood where I was going and what I needed to do.

Understanding different elements of my dream became apparent the more I worked with my students in the classroom. The dream images were symbolic messages of the way I wanted to handle my approach to teaching, taking into consideration the emotional and practical attitude each student brought to the classroom expressed through their creative development. The important elements of the dream, as indicated by the car (an instrument that moves us through daily life), the road (suggesting the right direction taken), the mountains (rising in awareness), the lake (calming the emotional life and becoming sensitive to everything around us), the birds (the ability to soar with freedom and to be playful), and the valley (the opening of new opportunities and direction), helped clarify my ability to instruct and reach students on their level of artistic cultivation.

In a Biblical, Old Testament view, the dream expression reminded me of a wise message found in the Book of Proverbs. "Prepare your work outside, get everything ready for you in the field; and after that build your house." (Proverbs 24: 27) This proverb could figure in any number of growth situations, but in this case, I looked at it as an avenue for structuring my teaching style. The dream symbols provided the coded subconscious raw material needed to alert me to the way I wanted to provide instruction on a conscious level. Once I clarified how I wanted to give clear lessons, provide time and room for the students to explore their creativity, and work with them individually, I could build a teaching style that was unique and expressly my own. But as all dreams "sound out" a general feeling of direction, and not an exact map of success, I discovered my teaching provided numerous success stories, as well as the occasional failure, as any teacher will attest to.

The most surprising element found in the dream concerned the playful antics of the birds that soared over the lake. As a teacher attached to my students and their projects, it became apparent that being playful in the classroom was an important ingredient to the creative mix. This was not the competitive play of organized sports, football playoffs or basketball tournaments, but the individual play of pupils free to explore their uniqueness as people and as artists. Playfulness became the background support for all the work that developed in the classroom. Almost everyday I was pleasantly surprised to witness, in little ways, the emerging talents and personalities of students who first presented themselves as uncreative candidates who quickly matured with expression, humor and play.

Diane Ackerman, a prolific writer concerned with the human condition, who probes the depth of our senses and our hearts, touches upon the theme of frolicsome activity. In her book, <u>Deep Play</u>, she addresses how much play is an active ingredient in our everyday lives.

> "The spirit of deep play is spontaneity, discovery, and being open to new challenges. As a result, it allows one to happily develop new skills, test one's limits, stretch them, and then maybe refine the skills and redefine the limits. What is its biological purpose? Not basic survival. It carries one across fear and uncertainty toward the slippery edges of possibility, where one must use oneself fully and stretch human limits to achieve the remarkable. It encourages discovery and growth. At first that feels thrillingly satisfying, but tedium sets in and we're soon eager for more, for something requiring greater skills, greater risk, newer challenges. One can see how important this trait might be in our own evolution. A new scheme, thrilling at first, rapidly becomes ordinary, and finally dull. Craving more moments of deep play, we set bigger challenges, develop new skills, take greater chances, canvass worlds." (Pgs. 38-39)

With cravings of deep play resounding in heads and hearts, I want to look at two affirmations of play structured into the active life of a long practicing studio artist/jeweler and a radio broadcast team that have delighted national audiences for years. Then at the conclusion of this last chapter of the book I will analyze each one of the chapter projects with former students who felt they couldn't draw a straight line with a ruler, but found happily that they could, overcoming alternative voices, personal adversity, and fear.

Finding A Voice of Her Own

To know Lucia is to know how much playfulness is an active part of her life. She is an accomplished businesswoman with a jewelry studio where clients linger in her outer-office pouring over an immense variety of individual gems, rings, bracelets, and necklaces. The alacrity in her office suggests more of a party atmosphere than a business meeting between proprietress and clients. Energetic laughter, hugs, and stories shared by both parties proceed before sincere business dealings are confirmed. Lucia's studio is unique, not the mall type of store where generic jewelry pieces can be found in abundance. The secret to her success is that she is the creator of all the unique jewelry pieces found in her studio that are so much in demand. From initial scratch paper sketches to the finished product Lucia's work is of the highest quality, demonstrated by her repeat business and requests from local galleries for her work.

But Lucia's creativity doesn't stop at jewelry making. Quite often when the stress and strain of her business gets to her she simply shifts gears and finds other outlets to keep her fresh and contented. Her other passion is singing and playing the guitar. As she explains, "my attentiveness to jewelry making and playing the guitar began in junior high school when

I turned fourteen. I needed to find an outlet to escape my dysfunctional family life. My parents fought constantly while my sister and I staged our own form of passive/aggressive behavior that contrasted the irrational and destructive tension that constantly lingered in our home."

"I began to hang with some students at school who had a fringe band and I became interested in their music, and particularly the guitars they played. One of my friends loaned me an old guitar and I began playing. The elemental sounds and chords were less than acceptable, but I kept at it. As I played, I began singing songs that were popular at the time and concluded that my voice was the stronger of the two disciplines. But I was ostracized and criticized by the boys in the group who looked down on my new found interest because, as they so vocally put it,...'Girls don't play guitars!' "

In high school Lucia was a steady and focused art student taking all the jewelry classes she could fit into her busy school schedule and taking guitar lessons on weekends. She thought she was making progress with her music, but the band members thought otherwise. Their haranguing continued. "I was particularly ridiculed," Lucia continues," and told not to play many of the songs that I was learning. In their own sing-song voices they would pass judgment saying…"don't play this, play that," and "don't sing like that, sing like this!" I thought I had the support of my girlfriends who hung around with the band but soon learned that their comments were wrapped in sarcasm. Their condescending voices hit me hard,…"hey Lucia, that's a cutesy song,..sing it, play it, that's a cutesy song!"

"So for the remainder of high school my interest in guitar playing took a back seat to my classroom studies and perfecting my jewelry skills. In college my interest in music continued but I still didn't receive the kind of support I was looking for. My degree work in jewelry kept me buoyed but there were feelings of inadequacy lingering at the edges of my consciousness. I felt passion for my art work but I suffered because I wanted that playfulness and passion to include my guitar playing and singing as well. It seemed like the music and art complemented each other and made me feel complete. After all the rejection, I needed someone to tell me it was okay to play on my own and enjoy the sounds I was creating!"

Years later as an adult with a thriving jewelry business and active family life, Lucia still managed to play her guitar and sing but, as she says, it was always "from the shadows" of her life. But a synchronistic event took place in her life that changed all that. While visiting musician friends at a party in a nearby city, Lucia was asked to join in and play with the band. She was hesitant at first, but found herself strapping on her guitar, playing, and adding her own vocal adaptation to the music. "One of the band members, a long time woman friend, came up to me after the session and complemented me on my soft playing and vocal rendition. I was momentarily speechless, but eventually thanked her for her comment. I said it was the first time in a long time that anyone took notice of my musical ability since I began playing back in junior high school."

"To my surprise, in front of my husband and the rest of the band members, my friend looked me straight in the eye, saying,…'Lucia, you need to find your own voice!' The metaphor was not lost on me. It was the first sign of affirmation and release to truly be myself washing away the years of negative comments that held me back from acceptance. But her comments didn't stop there. She turned to my husband, the gifted musical voice in our family, stating that he needed to acquiesce and share his singular singing position allowing Lucia's voice to blend into the family, to sing and play on her own merits. My husband wholeheartedly agreed, not only accepting and sharing my voice with his, but assisting me in locating and purchasing the right guitar to complement my singing."

"Since that pivotal day, I experience and give in to the playful vitality within myself, strumming chords and singing with passion! Not only am I more sure of who I am as a creative person, the visual and performing artist, but I have an affinity with many of my contemporaries who have given their professional lives to the advancement of women's voices in the field of music. Joni Mitchell comes to mind, as does, Shawn Colvin and Bonnie Raitt. My final joy is that, on occasion, my husband and I join together blending our voices as we play at home or before others, knowing that my playfulness and passion are fully expressed and fully alive."

Click and Clack, The Tappet Brothers

Playfulness generates numerous benefits throughout our active lives. Laughter, a natural by-product of creative amusement, massages our inner person, dismissing the tension that builds within our bodies. Laughter squeezes the facial muscles releasing the body's natural relaxant called beta-endorphins, abbreviated from 'endogenous morphine,' which means a morphine produced naturally throughout the body. This natural drug is pumped throughout the body easing tension, improving mood levels and protecting the immune system by blocking Cortisol, an immune system suppressant. Exercise, including playfulness and passionate activities, will release beta-endorphin activity, increasing the benefits of a healthful life. The next story about two Boston car mechanics makes full use of beta-endorphin activity as they dispense humorous car-care advise to people all across the country who phone in to their radio program asking advice to resolve their unique and unresolved car problems.

For sheer zaniness of spirit, National Public Radio's broadcast of Car Talk holds the prize. Each and every weekend car owners from across the country tune in their radios for an hour of laughter and playfulness with Click and Clack, The Tappet Brothers. In reality, Click and Clack are the brother team of Tom and Ray Magliozzi, the Martha Stewarts of fastidious car mechanics with a Marx Brothers style. They delight their audiences with car knowledge and car repair information dispensed with considerable rollicking laughter and slap stick humor. The program operates in a basic manner not unlike other talk shows where the radio audience is an important ingredient in the success of the broadcast.

The program includes a unique way of addressing callers and their car problems. When the brothers ask for the caller's name and location, which varies widely throughout the United States and Canada, Tom and Ray usually spend a minute or two playing with their name and the town they live in. Both of the brothers banter about the fact that they were, at some time or other, in the callers "fair city," and find something humorous to say about the town followed by peals of laughter. The car problem, for which the caller was making a request, seems not to be at all important at the moment. It's apparent right from the start that callers need to be in the right frame of mind to put up with the air wave mechanics shenanigans.

Despite the carefree atmosphere and getting off the subject a good deal of the time, Tom and Ray manage to bestow a great deal of helpful automotive information.

One of the qualities of their mechanical genius is asking questions of the caller about their car's adverse behavior. The questions are asked in such a way by both the brothers that lend a sense of mystery to the program. A listener has the feeling that they have tuned in to an audio version of *Murder On The Orient Express*. Tom and Ray's probing questions usually bring forth recognizable clues and robust "AH-HA" responses that occasionally raise cross diagnostic and conflicting answers from each brother, but each resolving in the end, the car's problem to the satisfaction of the caller.

One of the humorous effects of the Magliozzi Brothers car-side manner is to ask callers if their car makes particularly troublesome noises. Callers, without hesitation, are all too happy to mimic their vehicle's baneful sounds. With degrees of accuracy and vocal clarity, callers demonstrate squeaks, screeches, grinds, growls, clicks, bumps, thumps, and tapping sounds to help in the problem-solving. This audience participation also increases the level of laughable situations, leaving the brothers, the caller, and the radio audience chuckling, snickering, and guffawing at the variety of sounds that are made. Despite the silliness these audio sound effects make, Tom and Ray can readily find remedies based on the sound the car is emitting. In the end, more often than not, they leave their audience laughing as well as satisfied that the car owner's problems have been solved.

The brothers Magliozzi are not only highly regarded car

mechanics, but infinitely creative radio show hosts who add new material so their program doesn't become predictable and boring. While the main focus of the call-in program centers on cars and car repair, the addition of playful activities keeps the program fresh and stimulating. For instance, an amusing diversion called "stump the chumps"is a playful attempt to test the repair expertise of the two mechanics. Upon giving an answer for a difficult car problem the brothers ask the caller if he or she would like to return to the program several months hence to report if their car diagnosis and repair advice was correct. Not wanting to spoil the fun, the caller agrees. So with anticipation the caller and air wave mechanics reconnect with the usually positive response that Tom and Ray did, indeed, come up with the correct automotive solution followed, of course, by more laughter and chatter with the caller. But there is the rare occasion when a misdiagnosis is made and the brothers use this as an opportunity to reevaluate their diagnosis and learn that car repair doesn't always follow logical and predictable patterns, all couched in continual good humor.

Partway through Tom and Ray's hour long program, they take a break from addressing car owners and their problems to concentrate on "the puzzler,"a riddle designed to pique the enigmatic interest of listeners. The puzzler is given more emphasis and drama as one brother reads the challenging story to the other brother who listens attentatively, adding dramatic verbal statements like, "wow, that's a tough one to figure out," or, "M-A-N, where did you find this puzzle? I don't think anyone could POSSIBLY guess the right answer," followed by, "but I think I know the answer! ha, ha, ha!" Serious listeners to the program have a week to come up with the right puzzler answer and prove that they are just as clever and playful as Tom and Ray. The warmth and humor continue as the answer is divulged for the previous week's puzzler, and the lucky listener who came up with the correct answer wins a memorable car care prize.

Tom and Ray carry their frolicsome attitude right to the end of their program and poke fun at themselves by announcing, "Well you have done it again! You have wasted another perfectly good hour with Click and Clack, the Tappet Brothers." As they announce the people responsible for the quality control aspect of their broadcast, they raise the level of their playfulness and enter a prankish mood with slight of mouth and a heavy play on words. The brothers read the credits whether the people announced have anything to do with the program or not. From a long list of credits here is a sample of humorous titles and corresponding names: the Accounts Payable Administrator is Imelda Czechs, the Assistant Customer Car Representative is Kurt Reply, the Car Stereo Installer is Carlos Antenna, the Chief Estimator is Edward James Almost, the Chief of Tire Technology is Yessir Itsaflat, the Construction Manager is Dustin Dubree, the Customer Car Care Representative is Haywood Jabuzoff, the Director of Delicate Electronics Repair is Anita Hammer, and the Staff Bouncer is Euripedes Ibrakauface, just to name a few.

Tom and Ray Magliozzi prove to us every weekend on Car Talk that creative energy doesn't have to be taxing and a mystery trying to find an avenue for expression. Through humor the body and mind relax into procreative possibilities. Allowing playfulness to enter into the common area of an individual's activity encourages our inner energy to be released in ways we thought not possible. Lucia, as we saw, is a very playful person who found her creative potential demanded by her interior insistence to play the guitar, despite the years of criticism for following her passion, and later to be confirmed and encouraged by a good friend. It is important to note here that these two stories are about people who took the opportunity to be enablers. Click and Clack made operational the use of laughter for the benefit of listeners' inner well being while at the same time teaching and educating them of the wisdom of proper car care. A good friend sanctioned Lucia's music and enabled her to find that new voice that she knew was part of her.

Enablers represent the positive "other voices" that counteract the destructive words and statements that have tripped up our potential to be creative and productive. Those individuals who make an investment on our behalf have the wisdom and integrity to instruct and point us in the right direction. They may be teachers, coaches, relatives, or good friends who have our best interest at heart. These persons of influence find unique ways to dispense their knowledge, present opportunities to try out our emerging selves, and find the means to allow us to grow in a healthy environment. Jesus, the greatest enabler of all, used his empowerment entrusted from God, to influence everyone he came in contact with during his travels and ministry on earth. To his Disciples—and I use the word inclusively beyond Biblical examples to include contemporary men, women, and children—Jesus taught with authority that we all have the ability to go beyond ourselves and complete greater works. Set in a Christian context, it has a humanitarian position as well, the compassionate devotion to individual self-expression expanded outwardly toward the advancement of human welfare.

Investing in Commodities

Author and historian, Mike Dash, has documented the worldwide history of the tulip trade in his national bestseller, <u>Tulipomania: The Story of the World's Most Coveted Flower and the Extraordinary Passions it Aroused.</u> Throughout his book the author chronicles the movement of the tulip trade over a period of several centuries from the Tien Shan Mountains, an inhospitable area that defines the border between Russia, China, Tibet and Afghanistan, then moving through Turkey, Europe, and into the United Provinces of the Netherlands in the 1570's. The tulip's simply defined beauty created passionate responses from kings and potentates all along the Silk Trade Route, culminating in the frenzied hysteria of buying and selling of bulbs by Dutch gardening connoisseurs and merchants that reached a fever pitch by the 1630's. The Dutch created a business phenomenon: the marketing of tulip bulbs that had the potential for providing incredible beauty as well as forming the basic forerunner of a commodities stock market. Mike Dash explains it this way.

> "By agreeing to purchase bulbs that would not be ready for delivery for several months, the tulip traders had created what would today be called a futures market – simply defined, a form of speculation in which a dealer gambles on the future price of some commodity, whether it be flower bulbs or oil, by promising to pay a specified price for the goods on a fixed date sometime in the future. This was an event of some historical significance. In the 1630's the whole concept of futures was still a novelty. The very earliest

futures markets had been organized in Amsterdam less than thirty years earlier, the invention of merchants who traded in timber, hemp, or spices on the Dutch stock exchange. Tulips were the first commodity to be bought and sold outside the markets of Amsterdam, and the first to be traded by anyone other than high-ranking merchants and stock exchange specialists." (Pgs. 115-116)

While people are not tulip bulbs to be bought and sold, they still have the extraordinary potential for creative amplification, a useful commodity for an exceptional life. The beauty of the flowering tulip is hidden within the biological cell structuring of the bulb. With the right amount of growing time supported by soil, sun, water, temperature, and fertilizer, the tulip displays its visual gift to us. Likewise the human potential for growth is developed through support, encouragement, instruction, appreciation, patience, practice, and planted in a nurturing environment. While tulips bloom in the spring after laying dormant for most of the year, individuals slumber in the mentor/student relationship gaining a perspective on the kind of life they want to lead and the shaping of their talent.

Perhaps with the exception of the franchised professional athlete, the futures price of the human commodity cannot be fixed on a monetary scale. Belief in self and pride of workmanship are the qualities that make up the creative person in public work or private practice. So for those individuals who are struggling with emotional energy on the pathway to shaping their creativity, the next five narratives should provide some encouragement for their efforts. These stories are examples of students I influenced, both young and old, who risked themselves in an effort to work beyond the concept of "not being able to draw a straight line with a ruler!" Their stories represent struggles matched with considerable success, and the occasional disappointment, but the important thing is each student tried and achieved a level of competency and enjoyment in a learning experience. The stories include a young Hispanic youth transplanted from a large inner-city trying to escape gang activity, an elderly grandmother looking for a creative outlet, a high school basketball star looking for a non-credit art class before he graduates, a young girl looking for a safe classroom activity to escape a dysfunctional home life, and a beautiful young scholar who wanted to excel in the creative arts as much as she excelled in her other studies. Each of these individuals forged new creative energy through the introduction of the design projects included at the end of each chapter of this book.

#1 Graffiti to Graph Paper Designs

Antonio appeared in my classroom three weeks after the first quarter of the school year began. By the time he was escorted into my art class by the vice-principal, my students were well into their first assignment painting a still-life carefully staged in the center of the room. The energy of the students, which had been centered on stretched canvases arranged on easels all about the room, was suddenly diverted to the young boy standing by the door. Antonio looked like someone from another world. He was young, a fourteen year old Hispanic whose physical presence suggested the diminutive height and weight of a horse racing jockey. He wore baggy black pants pulled tight at the ankles and tied tight above white NIKE running shoes with a red swoosh. Antonio wore a black long sleeved shirt covered with a gray sleeveless Oakland raiders sweatshirt. His black hair was pulled back and tightly wrapped in a bun and covered by a dark hair net. The fingers of each of his hands were covered with letter and small tattoo symbols. Antonio was a gang member.

Antonio was removed from a South Los Angeles environment to protect him from retribution from his own gang members for wanting to escape the violent street life that ruled his existence. But like the witness protection program, Antonio was shuffled from one school to the next in an effort to cover his trail and avoid detection. He looked physically tired and the expression on his face suggested both fear for the life he left behind and apathy toward his present transient movements. The vice-principal said that Antonio had some artistic aptitude but wouldn't fit into my advanced painting class because he may be moved again in a few weeks. His advice was to give him some paper and a pencil, place him in the corner of the room, and let him express his feelings, drawing whatever he felt like. I bristled at the thought of abandoning Antonio to the outer edge of the classroom, ostracizing him away from the warmth and positive energy experienced by my other students.

Antonio proved to be a punctual student, showing up for class everyday, sitting in the corner of the room, drawing continuously on scraps of paper. For a while he drew only one subject from memory, gang related scenes. The pages were filled with pencil drawings of hand guns, knives, custom low rider cars, scenes of drive by shootings, gang signs and gang clothing. Sometimes he scribbled graffiti words along the sides of the pages like documented notes of past scenes in his young life. For the remainder of the quarter Antonio never spoke to me or any of the students in my class. My students reciprocated, either out of respect for his need to be alone, or perhaps out of embarrassment for not knowing how to approach him and get to know him.

As the first quarter ended and the second quarter began, I didn't expect to see Antonio again, anticipating that I would hear from the vice-principal that he had been moved to another school some distance away. But to my surprise Antonio was the first one to arrive in class, moving directly to his corner of the room and getting right to work. He acknowledged me for the first time but verbal exchanges between us were yet to take place. During the brief break between quarters I put up numerous examples of graph paper designs completed by students from another class. For the remainder of that class day, while my students painted diligently on their canvases, Antonio walked back and forth in front of the graph designs mounted on the classroom wall. He was self absorbed, caught up in myriad examples of designs repeating themselves over and over again until the eyes become blurred in sensory overload.

As Antonio gazed at the wall of design work, I cautiously moved in his direction. He sensed my presence and turned to face me. I asked him if he would be interested in creating some designs like the ones displayed on the wall. His expression changed somewhat as he shook his hand affirming his interest in the graph paper design project. I found several sheets of graph paper for him to experiment on and carefully instructed him on how the design sequence takes shape. Before I completed my instruction he was already applying pencil to paper, not ignoring what I was saying, but intent on testing his creativity energy. By the end of the class Antonio had several five square unit designs to work with, each holding promise for completed design projects. As the bell rang for my students to move on to their next class, Antonio collected his graph paper designs, storing them in his folder instead of his art locker, and walked out the door.

When Antonio returned to class the next day he placed the graph paper designs in front of me as I sat at my desk and then stood there without saying a word. I was surprised by the beauty of each one of the designs. In our strange symbiosis to try and understand one another without speaking, I smiled, got up from my desk with his work in hand, and walked to the wall and stapled his designs next to the student work already on display. After we both admired his achievements, Antonio found more graph paper, located some colored pencils, and went back to work on more designs. Apparently satisfied with what he had already designed he began to include symbols and shapes from his gang past with new shapes of creative interest. Graffiti shapes were woven into the square unit free-form designs and enhanced with the use of color applied to several areas of the graph paper. The work was startling and dramatic. Not only was I watching his work with interest but many of my advanced design and painting students were gathering at the display wall to study his designs.

Trying to understand Antonio's feelings toward his design work was difficult at best. Our interactions were like playing charades without words. I had to concentrate on his body language to get a reading on his sensibilities. When he first arrived in class there was no animation to his presence; he stared at the floor, his shoulders inclined forward, his eyes darted from side to side, he sat with his back to the class, and his focal point remained centered on the art paper in front of him. As time passed and he became absorbed in the graph patterns, his appearance brightened and his energy level intensified as he found a new avenue of self expression. Perhaps he found peace within himself from the difficult and fearful life he left behind.

With time, I thought Antonio's voice would find its range and evidence of his feelings would be revealed. Unfortunately, that didn't happen. One day in the middle of the second quarter, the vice-principal informed me that Antonio was removed from his classes and sent to a school in another state. He was shifted to another location so quickly that he didn't have time to clear out his locker and take his design projects with him. I can only speculate that Antonio felt supported during his brief stay and found a creative outlet that would buoy his self-esteem and improve his outlook on life. I have kept his work in a collection of past student work and get it out occasionally to show new students the power and descriptive accuracy demonstrated as samples for their own beginnings. I think of Antonio occasionally and hope his transient school life ended and he is a productive, stable person shaped somewhat by the free-form designs that he experienced in my classroom.

#2 Questions With the Circle and Line Design

Estelle was the total opposite of Antonio in active mannerisms and vocal declarations. While Antonio said nothing, Estelle said everything. She was an elderly widow who was looking for new direction and vitality to fill the void left in her life when her husband died. Estelle had enrolled in my evening painting class at the community college, joining a cross section of students: advanced placement high school students, drop out students fulfilling their GED, and an assemblage of adults at various levels of painting skill. And while most of my new students came with painting supplies and an attitude to work, Estelle seemed more interested in meeting new people and striking up conversations.

The first class session was taken up with my usual introductory remarks, passing out a class syllabus, art supply list, and making out a roll sheet placing students names with faces and identifying more quickly with their work. I ambled along explaining my method of instruction, encouraging student self expression, and making sure they understood that I would be available for one-on-one assistance. It was the "one-on-one" assistance that Estelle zeroed in on from the very beginning. As the introductory class session ended and the students prepared to leave, Estelle moved in my direction with a barrage of questions. "I know nothing about painting, will you give me plenty of help?" *Yes, of course.* "What do I do, how do I get started?" *Begin by reading the syllabus and follow the basic information.* "Where do I buy the art supplies?" *Art supply stores and addresses are listed on the supply sheet I handed out.* "What should I paint?" *We can discuss subject matter during the next class meeting.* "Other students already know how to paint. Am I in the right class?" *Yes, students work independently and at their own level.*

By the time I put my own material away, moved toward the classroom door, turned out the lights and locked the door, Estelle had asked a half-dozen more questions that let me know explicitly of her insecurity concerning her ability to paint for the first time. While she wore her emotions tensely on her sleeve, I intuitively felt that she was carrying a burden on her shoulders as well, a burden that came to light during the second week of instruction. During the next class session Estelle was unable to make a clear commitment toward a beginning painting project. She dabbled with her paint, tried several attempts at drawing from a still life, walked around the room in a restless manner looking at other student work and talking incessantly. Despite the help I offered her, nothing productive came of our combined efforts. Clearly I needed a different approach in calming her down and gaining her trust so she could find some security and freedom to work on her own.

At the end of class, before Estelle could bombard me with more searching questions, I sat down with her to probe with my own carefully stated question to find out what her fears were surrounding her inability to begin painting. For the first time since she arrived in class she became very quiet, losing her mask of gregariousness, looking down at the work table in sadness as if I had found the weak spot in her character and exposed it to the world. After a painfully prolonged minute of silence, she began to confide in me the obstacles that were holding her back from really expressing herself.

"When I was a child some of my friends dared me to jump off the high dive at a nearby lake one summer," Estelle began. "They kept at their request so long that I became embarrassed. It seemed like everyone at the lake was staring at me, and the pressure to jump became intense. So I climbed up the diving ladder and stood at the edge of the high dive and stared down at the water. The height was too great and I couldn't take the plunge. I climbed down the ladder, swam to shore and left the lake hearing the taunts of my friends behind me. My life at that point, and forever after, was shaped by that childhood experience. Every time I was presented with a new or challenging possibility in my life I discovered I couldn't follow through. I always sought safety, and rejected risk in my life. For forty-five years my husband kept me in safety. He managed my life wonderfully, but since his death I have had to find new ways to manage my own life. In many respects I feel that this class is a real risk for me. I see myself standing on the diving tower again deciding whether I can take the plunge. I am nervous, anxious, and feeling very inadequate surrounded by the accomplished work of the students in class. I've thought of quitting but I need to get by this feeling; I just don't know where to go from here."

As I sat with Estelle, listening to her story, I could feel her pain and inner turmoil. After some words of support, I suggested to her that we take a different approach. I indicated that what I had in mind was for her to jump off the lower deck instead of climbing the tower only to stare down into the water. "Instead of painting," I suggested, "let's begin by creating some simple circle and line design patterns." I took a piece of paper and began drawing a circle and four lines of equal length. Then I carefully explained how the lines interact with the circle to form a creative free-form, abstract design. "Since the design is small and manageable, you can control what you place on the page. Different patterns will emerge that may be of interest to you. If not, make more small designs until you find something that pleases you," I concluded. The new approach of placing recognizable elements together gave Estelle a chance to get started, breaking her penchant of not taking a risk in new endeavors.

Before I had a chance to completely close up the classroom

for the evening, Estelle had drawn a number of interesting shapes. Pleased with what she had accomplished, her conversable attitude returned and so did her penchant to ask questions. "Can I take my drawings home and create more of them?" *Of course, draw as many as you like.* "Can I color areas of the designs?" *That would be a good direction to take next. Use colored pencil, paint can come later.* "Can I make the designs larger?" *Certainly!* As we walked down the hall and out into the parking lot her excitement and questions continued, and I began to chuckle. "What," she said, "what's so funny?" "You are," I said with enthusiasm. "I think you just climbed the diving tower and took your first plunge. How does it feel? "Wonderful," was her parting comment as we headed for our cars to head home. Estelle made steady progress during the course of the art class eventually trading in her small designs to begin a painting on canvas board. Over time her nervous energy was replaced by an emerging confidence to take risks in new projects and all the questioning gradually faded into manageable classroom work experience. I didn't see Estelle after that pivotal class, but I was of the opinion that she was out in the world finding new challenges and testing her ability to metaphorically leap off diving towers with creative ease.

#3 Moods and Tangrams

Kelly was the first student to enter my classroom each day. She always knew I would be at my table top podium at the front of the room checking my notes for class and preparing to take roll. She would pop her head in the door before entering and ask the same question she always asked, "Are you in a good mood today?" "Yes," I would respond, "I'm in a good mood today!" Where upon she would walk into class content that I had responded with the right password somehow guaranteeing her a successful day of work. As the school year progressed, and the same pre-class question continued, I began to consider her motive for presented herself in such a way. What if, I speculated, I said I was not in a good mood. What then? What was behind her question that I needed to always be in a good mood for her?

So one morning as Kelly and I went through the question and answer routine, I approached her and said, "just out of curiosity, Kelly, what would happen if I said I was in a bad mood?" Her response was very quick, caustic and uncharacteristic. Her typically lighthearted attitude became dark and overcast as she answered, "you always have to be in a good mood, you just have to. Don't even think about being in a bad mood!" I was taken back by her sudden change in attitude but before I could pursue the matter further, other students entered the classroom so I dropped the issue. Later during the day I checked in with Kelly's counselor to see if some light could be shed on her background and her sudden change in behavior. The counselor gave a portrayal of Kelly's family as extremely dysfunctional, alcoholic parents, an older brother in jail as a felon, a suicidal sister, family fights carried out in their broken down trailer in the woods, family always in debt, and dismantled cars throughout the yard where Kelly would retreat to escape all the verbal and physical abuse. "Kelly," the counselor concluded, "arrives very early to school each day and stays just as long as she can to avoid going home to her impaired and monstrous home life."

The following day, after Kelly and I exchanged our "good mood" question and response routine, I told her that I apologized for upsetting her so easily the previous day. Without any malice in her voice she divulged the reason she barked at me. "My home life is so crazy and chaotic that I need a place where I can function in some sort of normal atmosphere. I need a place where I know I can work without threats and intimidation and feel real comfort to be myself. That's why I always ask if you are in a good mood. If your day is going badly, my day will go badly too. I realize it's an unreal expectation to always have you be in a good mood everyday but without it my day disintegrates and I don't feel safe." I thanked her for her candor saying, "occasionally I am not in a good mood, but we can continue to declare our mood rehearsal check-in and make this a safe place for the both of us." The conversation was an intimate verbal bonding experienced by the both of us for the rest of the school year.

 Kelly was a good art student enrolled in my advanced design course. She had a natural flair and understanding for the principles of art, the creative organization of design shapes, and understood compatible color combinations and arrangements. At the time of our conversation she was working on an independent study project with tangram designs. She had completed several tangram patterns, sectioned off the proper seven shapes and was preparing to cut each tangram puzzle into individual pieces and arrange them into different design patterns. Without trying to be a classroom therapist I asked her if she had a direction for her design considerations. "What do you mean?," she responded. I thought for a moment, carefully considering my train of thought, and continued. "You are creating something new with shape and space. You have also confided in me the emotional pattern of your family structure that so affects your moods and behavior. You might consider treating some of your new designs as an emotional response to the way you see your family. Other designs you might arrange in a way that represents your feelings of how you see yourself separate of the upheaval within your family."

Kelly studied me with an expression on her face that seemed to indicate that I was completely nuts! "How do I do that," she blurted out. Instead of explaining what I was asking her to do, I took one of her tangram designs, cut the pieces apart, and began arranging the units across a larger piece of dark paper as a way to contrast the white triangles, square and rhamboid. Although some of the pieces touched points and sides in a different way, the design no longer resembled a tangram. Kelly could see immediately what I was doing. With new intent she took over my layout and began to rearrange the pieces to meet her own creative desire. Her energy increased throughout the period as she cut up more tangrams and added a series of original designs to her independent project before the class concluded for the day.

Kelly's independent project continued for another three weeks without any direction or suggestions on my part. She was thoroughly engrossed in her design work and confident of the direction her work was taking. Somehow my suggestions gave her a new found sense of freedom to be productive, working out some entangled family issues with paper pieces pasted on backing board, colors highlighting certain designs, and some designs layered with multiple thickness of materials adding a dimensional relief. At the end of the project she turned in a dozen of her best visual schemes, and together, we placed them on the gallery wall in the classroom. The work made a bold and creative statement.

I didn't feel the need to pry into Kelly's new independent

attitude and liberated confidence, because I became aware of her new entrance into class each day. With her new self-reliant attitude in place, she dismissed the need to ask me if I was in a good mood. Instead, our roles were reversed as I playfully asked her, "Kelly, are you in a good mood today?" "Yes," she would repeat as she moved toward her art locker to get art work out, "I'm in a good mood today!"

#4 Basketball and Kaleidoscopes

Darren was his name but everyone who knew him called him "Buff," short for Buffalo. It was the perfect nickname that matched his physical appearance. Buff's movements were slow and unruffled and he carried his presence with shoulders rounded forward, his hands thrust deep in his pockets. He walked forward on the balls of his feet suggesting that he could fall forward at any moment. As Buff moved along in his gentle manner, his disheveled crop of tightly curled hair, flowing evenly to his shoulders, bounced along in a uniform rhythm. He had a soft voice and measured his words thoughtfully before speaking. His disposition was tempered with a dry sense of humor, and he always seemed to have an altruistic interest in the students that sought his attention.

Buff's languorous appearance belied his true gift as a high school basketball star. He held several achievements for high school and state shooting records: the most points scored in league play, the most points scored in tournament play, and the highest assists for any player in a season. On the basketball floor, Buff shed his indolent manner assuming the position of a smart, quick moving guard who possessed a graceful and elegant jump shot, hitting the basket often from almost any range, driving the opposing teams crazy. During his junior year, college scouts were often seen in the stands, keeping track of his progress, and letters of inquiry arrived daily from schools who could put his talent to work quickly, with offered scholarships to back up their interest in him. By the beginning of his senior year, Buff had completed all but two of his high school credits required for graduation. This left him with the option to take some electives to round out his remaining class schedule.

I got to know Buff personally one day when he wandered into my classroom, introduced himself, and inquired about my design and painting classes. He had indicated an interest in creative expression but never found the time to get involved with the fine arts because basketball and academic courses had taken up all his time. He thought a couple of art classes would be fun to take helping him relax and enjoy working in some creative mediums. From experience, I knew that by this time "senioritis" was a serious disease that afflicted most students who were closing in on the end of their high school careers. I was sure he was looking for a couple of easy courses to take to coast through the rest of the school year. Little did I know that Buff would prove me wrong.

Buff signed up for my basic design course as well as a primary painting class. His easy manner belied some apprehension he felt getting started with art projects. "Basketball and sports in particular have always come naturally to me," he remarked the first day of class, "but I don't think I will be scoring high with art." To get started I introduced him to the circular kaleidoscopic design suggesting that he create some simple design patterns that would bolster his confidence and not reflect on his lack of artistic skill. Once I explained to him, and the rest of the class, the procedures of the project and showed plenty of examples, I stood back and let them begin.

Surprisingly Buff dived right into the project without a second thought applying energy that seemingly brought form to the overused sports cliche – when the going gets tough, the tough get going! He worked at fever pitch, creating design after design, but discarded each creation as quickly as he produced them. Buff seemed satisfied with his energy output, but ambivalent about his designs. When I approached him he seemed agitated. "I don't know what's wrong. I don't like anything I've drawn, and it's making me anxious." I sat with him, studying the designs, appraising his emotional concerns. "Buff," I began, "creative work is not like racking up baskets and keeping track of stats at the end of a basketball game. Creating designs is quite often a hit and miss affair that takes time and consideration. Be kind to yourself, slow down, relax, and let some of the designs speak to you by studying what you've created. Ruminate on your efforts for a time." Buff thought a moment. "You mean like a cow chewing its cud?" We both starting laughing. "Yeah," I concluded, "in a manner of speaking!" Buff continued to struggle with the design work over the remainder of the week as more and more designs continued to pile up. "Keep everything you've done," I advised, "because you may want to combine separate design elements together for a completed project."

Surprisingly, Buff had little difficulty with the painting class. Once again he threw all his energy into a new endeavor, but with less frenzy, and better results. Although he would struggle with the painting medium, it was his natural drawing style that flowered right from the beginning. He spent some time drawing a group of Holstein cows standing out in an open field. The drawing was superbly structured and the layout of the cows was well balanced on the canvas. But what made the drawing unique was the drawing style that Buff used to detail the work. He made small swirls with his pencil to indicate all the dark and light patterns of the scene. At close range the images became abstract circles that defied a recognizable format, but viewed from a distance, the appearance of the work took focus as a pastoral country scene. Buff was content with the one painting, working without pause on the project from beginning to end, drawing with ease and learning painting techniques with some instruction and considerable self direction. His painting style repeated the same drawing format, small brush strokes that curled in tight units that brings to mind the stylistic approach of Vincent Van Gogh's later work.

Eventually Buff solved his dilemma with the kaleidoscopic design, creating a wonderfully repeating circular pattern that was painstakingly painted, and when spun, created a mesmerizing range of blended colors. But now he had a new problem. "Why did I wait so long to get involved with art," he mumbled. "I graduate in six weeks and I've run out of time and classes to take. I've gotten hooked on painting, drawing, and design, but in the fall I will be in college studying business and concentrating on basketball." Buff's countenance languished as he spoke. "It doesn't have to be that way," I countered. "You can take elective courses in college to augment your required courses in business. Or you might consider art as a major, and minor in business. With your natural talent for painting and illustration you could combine the two disciplines and choose a career as a studio artist, free lance designer, or work in an advertising agency." Buff was listening to my counsel, but staring at a future that was already planned and programmed for him, and it didn't include art as a life focus. Buff continued to concentrate on numerous design and drawing assignments for the remaining six weeks of school. I worked with him on each piece of work, discussing techniques and giving encouragement, but from that point on we didn't discuss what shape his future would take.

Buff graduated with honors, both athletic and academic, but it would be years before I found out what direction his life would take. But one day in the middle of a beginning painting class, trying to keep my wits about me as I attended to the artistic needs of my fledgling painters, Buff walked casually through the door. It was the same old Buff, leaning slightly forward on the balls of his feet, hands thrust in the pockets of a fashionable business suit. His hair was cropped and styled, no longer the shaggy tight curls that spawned his nickname. "Buff," I stammered with surprise, "You look…so…businesslike! Do I still call you Buff, or are you beyond that name?" "No," he said in his quiet way, "I still go by Buff. They only call me Darren at my business." "Business!, what business?," I asked. "I'm an illustrator in Canada, working on independent assignments through a graphic design agency. "Wow," was my surprising reply, "I'm impressed!"

For the remainder of all my classes that day, Buff hung around and filled in the spaces of his life since leaving high school. He went on to college majoring in art instead of business and played basketball, setting more scoring records, but realizing that his athletic life would end once he graduated with his bachelor of fine arts degree. With his art portfolio in hand he headed to Canada where he has been ever since, immersed in creative illustrative assignments that mean so much more than the business world would have offered to him. I cherished his visit. In not so many words his visit to my classroom represented a belated thank you for the support and encouragement I offered him in shaping his direction. "In a way," he concluded, as we shook hands before we parted at the end of the day, "I'm still racking up stats. They aren't stats on the basketball court that didn't have much meaning for me after a certain period of time. They are stats for the completed illustrations that add to my resume and portfolio. It's the creative work that comes to me from my depth that is so satisfying." "Kudos," I said, as he walked away.

#5 Alicia's Maze

If there was ever a student dedicated to all aspects of art it was Alicia. She took every course I offered, from the time she entered as a Freshman right through her Senior year. Considering the difficulty of the required courses she crammed into her schedule, I was surprised that Alicia found the time to take all my basic and advanced drawing, painting, and graphic design classes. When Alicia ran out of electives she stretched herself further, creating a self directed independent study program complete with syllabus and daily lesson plans. But Alicia didn't quit there. Her focus continued as an advanced placement student in my adult evening program at the community college. She became such a fixture in my room, I was beginning to think we were related somehow. "Why all this intensity," I finally asked her. Her answer, like her work ethic, was direct and to the point. "I intend to continue in the footsteps of my father, and grandfather, who are both doctors," Alicia countered. "I want to study pre-med at

Stanford and continue on to UCLA for doctoral work in medicine, focusing particularly on medical illustration." I was duly impressed to say the least.

    Alicia was an exceptionally fine artist, with technical skill demonstrated in all her visual presentations. Her problem, as I sensed it, was not that she couldn't draw a straight line with a ruler, but rather could her ruler measure up to her forebears medical accomplishments. I understood some of her intensity to achieve on a high level because her father was my preferred physician. His professional manner was formal and reserved, his examinations thorough and complete. Alicia mirrored many of her fathers traits. She was small in stature, slim like her attentive physician father, beautiful, but modest, and exacting a meaningful determination to accomplish whatever she set her mind to. Like father, like daughter, I surmised.

    Her academic accumulative grade point average was a perfect 4.0 right through the first quarter of her Junior year. By the end of her second quarter of study I noticed that the quality of her art work in the painting class was not as strong as she had produced in the past. Instead of the usual A grade, I marked her computer grade sheet with an A-.

    Little did I know I was in for a stormy confrontation with Alicia for the slight demarcation. She marched into my class, rigid in appearance, her face fully flushed, demanding to know why I gave her such a low mark. Realizing a scene could be in the making I kept my tone relaxed and my voice down. "Your work hasn't been quite as strong this quarter as it has in the past. Two of your painting assignments were quite late, not meeting the deadlines required for the work to be handed in to me. We talked about this during the course of the class and you said you understood. Other than that your conduct has continued to be superior as always," I concluded. "But an A-," she blurted out, "I need an A!" "You do have an A", I countered, "just not as high as in the past,"a line not the least bit helpful. "But you don't understand," she said, as tears began to well up in her eyes, "an A- won't do me any good. The lowered grade will ruin my grade point average!"

As Alicia's tears flowed, I was beginning to understand the kind of pressure she had placed upon herself. As she stood before me it was apparent that the wheels on the vehicle that was going to carry her safely into the future, were falling off. The dominoes were tipping in her life. Without her saying so I could see where this was going. Without the perfect 4.0 grade point average Stanford wouldn't accept her into their pre-med program, doctoral work at UCLA would not be possible, and the accumulative disappointment from her family would be imagined as a dark cloud overshadowing her life. Feeling somewhat responsible for the difficulty facing her, I indicated that I was willing to make a concession on her behalf to bring the grade up to an A. "What?," she said, her appearance focusing immediately on the challenge. "I am willing to accept two design projects, of your own choosing, to be completed before the deadline for grade changes is due in the counseling office," I began. "You will have three weeks to complete the work. It means that the assignments will be in addition to the work you are currently completing in design class. So," I concluded, "this project will have to be considered homework. So let me know what you intend to do." "I already know," she hurriedly admitted. "I want to create two maze designs like the ones I completed in the beginning design class during my Freshman year." So off she went, the figurative dominoes being righted once again in her life, to design two-dimensional maze constructions. "If you build it, Stanford will come," I jokingly yelled after her.

Two weeks later, Alicia appeared in my classroom early in the morning before classes started, carrying her completed makeup projects. Both designs were exquisite. The designs were carefully thought out with trails leading in all directions to confuse and confound the viewer. Her color choices were richly brushed in without a single mistake, and the pathways were separated by contrasting hues giving the overall work a three-dimensional appearance. "That's not all," she said smiling. She directed me toward the hallway as her father entered the room carrying a three-dimensional model of one of the designs. She had taken the assignment one step further and created a maze with constructed and painted walls and pathways made out of stiff chipboard, a thin gray cardboard used for model construction. The chipboard construction was two inches high, scored, bent, and glued to a thick quarter inch piece of masonite. The whole work was suggestive of a miniature corn field, or hedgerow maze, without the plants and "Field of Dreams" baseball field.

As Alicia's father placed the maze construction on one of the classroom work tables, he began a lengthy commentary on Alicia's work ethic and future plans. Comments meant as much for my edification, as for her understanding. "You certainly must know by now that my daughter is a determined, independent, and focused individual, all of it mixed together at times to a fault. I'm not sure where all this relentless energy, or the need for perfection, comes from. Her mother and I have always supported her efforts, but we have not pushed her in any way to meet any forced standard of excellence, especially as a career in the medical profession. She is prideful and intent upon becoming a doctor to carry on the heritage of doctors within our family. Choosing the medical profession is admirable, but I'm hoping she will relax to a point and know that life has other options to look toward."

The message that Alicia and I heard that day didn't reach far enough. Her father meant well, speaking from the font of his experience, but it was apparent that Alicia's foundation was stuck in gear, anxiety created by the singular need to reach her one and only goal as a respected doctor and successful medical illustrator. Her reality was that she could draw, paint, and design multiple straight lines with any ruler she chose, and do it with ease. But she couldn't see, or come to terms with the singular notion that her art work offered her any joy, or that she could find those "ah-ha" experiences so necessary for creative energy and self discovery. Alicia could not find the, "ears to hear," or the,"eyes to see," as she continued to focus on the surface of her work as a by-product that would launch her into a prestigious university.

Her Senior year of studies continued in the same pattern, and once again we tangled with a reduced grade mid way through her second quarter. "You have an A, Alicia," I found myself saying again, "it just has a minus beside it." "I'll do another make-up assignment," she countered, as if to checkmate my remark. "That's not the point, Alicia," I said with some annoyance. "Receiving an A-, or God forbid, even a B will not end your life!" We went round and round with no resolution to the point I was trying to make, and two weeks later another make-up assignment appeared on my desk. Alicia was eventually accepted at Stanford and was happily speeding along on the course she had set for herself. The last time I saw her father for a physical he said he didn't know what to do with all

Alicia's art work that had piled up in the closet in her room. "Frame most of it and place it on the walls in your home. If she didn't appreciate it, you certainly can."

Postscript

SEEING THE POSSIBILITIES FROM WITHIN

*O Sower of seeds, how came you to prize
the beauty within that hid from my eyes?
O Sower of seeds,
the husk has been broken;
all praise to you for helping me open.*
                    Joyce Rupp, <u>Fresh Bread,</u>

When I think of Nelson Mandela, I imagine his incredible courage to endure countless years of imprisonment at the hands of the Apartheid government, and the patience to lead his people peacefully through governmental changes in South Africa. He has made some remarkable statements throughout his life, but one declaration he made in a public address in 1994 makes a strong point for the writing of this book.

Our deepest fear is not that we are inadequate. Our deepest fear is that we are powerful beyond measure. It is our light, not our darkness, that most frightens us. We ask ourselves, who am I to be brilliant, talented, fabulous? Actually, who are you not to be? You are a child of God. Your playing small doesn't serve the world....

In essence "your playing small" is a clear declaration representing the resultant condition that afflicts individuals throughout their lives. Playing small is that ugly state in which a person is shaped by separate utterances that capture the flag of creativity and hold people in bondage to self. As disenfranchised people curl in on themselves in their smallness, their own words help complete the "dumbing down" process. "I can't draw a straight line with a ruler" has been the headline by which all subheadings follow that say *I can't because I'm not worthy* ! In the last chapter I described some of the emotional effects that limited some of my students' ability to function creatively. Now the questions can be raised: What are the physical effects that suppress a person from lively individualism by the words and action of others? How does the body react to disingenuous harassment? A short story helps shape my point.

Recently, while on a business trip to New York City, I stood on a subway platform waiting for a connection to another part of town. Amid the press of people, the noise, and the hubbub of movement, my eye caught a young couple standing near a platform bench. The young man was trying to wrap himself around the girl like a snake in heat. Ah, young love, was my first response. But studying them more closely I discovered something distressing taking place. The man was animated, the woman was like cold stone. With his body pressed tightly against her, and his face directly against hers, he was speaking soft words one moment and harsh ones the next. Every time he tried to look directly into her eyes she would turn her head away from his gaze. Her expression was indifferent and lifeless. To try and get a reaction, he took her glasses, then her purse, holding them behind her back while he continued his dominant press against her. It became obvious that he was trying to tyrannize her into submission. As my connecting train arrived I spotted a policeman moving within range of the young couple. The scene was quickly lost to me as commuters and I gathered and the train pulled away from the platform.

The affect of words spoken in derision have a similar physical characteristic demonstrated by the young woman on the subway platform. Disrespectful expressions pierce the heart of the listener, and the wound is registered in the brain. Often times the face becomes flushed, and the eyes become pinched and downcast. The mind reels with the objectionable words, and the response is a toss-up between fight or flight. Confusion reigns as if you have just been shot from the bush, but you can't really see who is behind the bush. You know you have been hurt, but you become silent as the mind tries to comprehend why someone would hurt you in this way. You want to escape, but the objectionable comments come from someone you care about, or from an authority figure that shapes or controls your life. And because you do not, or cannot, retaliate, you back up. And as you back up, they move ahead with more remarks because they think you acquiesce to their authority, until you believe what they say as truth for your life. Then to keep the peace, you create your own version of someone else's falsehood and the damage is complete. That is the effect of verbal abuse. That is what a diminished life feels like. That is what playing small means!

To leave you small is not the intent of this book. Presenting yourself large to the world is the attitude presented here, not a post-mortem of a damaged existence. In the words of the Franciscan priest, Fr. Murry Bodo, "Sometimes we think our lives are ending, but they are really just beginning." So under the circumstances, how do we begin anew? To a degree this is a self help book, but hard and fast rules don't necessarily apply. What I do solicit however, is the quality that I keep presenting throughout the pages of this book: tapping your creative energy. Getting in touch with that conceptual intensity is like turning on a computer for the first time. All the menus and software available to the user present all kinds of possibilities for original productivity. But how does each person sort it all out? Well, I refer to the wise words of my computer savvy son who hints, "Dad, sometimes you just have to play with the computer systems to find out how they will work for you." Playfulness releases the body's tension, giving rise to a new sense of freedom to experiment with the unknown. Like the patient at the dental office who took a potent medication for a surgical procedure was heard to say," I still feel some pain, but I don't care." Playfulness has the same effect. The effects of the pain of playing small to self and the world linger, but spontaneous abandon in playful inventiveness emerge despite the persistent restraints placed around us. In a more carefree entitlement, one could surmise, it's time to "lighten up!"

Before we can play big to the world however, we must learn to play big with ourselves. This requires a safe environment, a generous dollop of courage, and a support system that allows each person to give rise to their creative potential. Imaging oneself in the category of a childlike activity such as applying colored chalk on a sidewalk in the summertime might be what's called for in this instance. Having a safe environment where courage can take root, and a support system that can be identified by those who are busily creating chalk-line shapes all around could support a statement that reads-creativity loves company!

Now moving the metaphor to a more realistic format, the scene could be arranged in a "classroom" setting where an individuals limited creative ability is gradually reduced in favor of a new confidence that builds within as each person learns new ways of developing a creative side. If what you discover about yourself brings forth those ever important "ah-ha" experiences, then you have stretched the boundaries of your life. A good example of this is a bumper sticker that I discovered recently with a decidedly Zen ring to it, that read, *I'd Rather Be Here, Now*! Creative self discovery is a here and now experience, not a wish into the future that may or may not take place. Once that process takes shape, then you become more aware of yourself in the world, and the world, quite often, becomes more aware of you.

A point can be made for the creative "here and now" experience through a story wonderfully described in an account between a dying grandmother and her granddaughter. Sara, a seven year old, accompanied her father to the hospital where they joined the rest of their family who were visiting her ailing grandmother. The grandmother, who had been ill for some time, took a turn for the worse and was not expected to live through the day. Before the father and daughter entered the hospital room, he took her aside with some cautionary comments. "Sara," he began, "I want you to be quiet and respectful when we enter the room, and stay out of the way of grandmother's bed. She is very ill and needs plenty of rest and quiet. Can you do that for me?" The girl, torn with feelings, was not sure how to answer. She responds instead with a nod, and they both enter the room.

Numerous family members were seated quietly around the bed. Grandmother was resting with her eyes closed, her head propped up slightly, with her arms placed across her stomach and hands clasped together. Sara was restless in the quiet of the room, and her love for her grandmother drew her closer to the bed. Despite her father's whispered protests, she moved to the side of the bed to get a clearer image of her dying grandmother. Within a few moments Sara reached out and touched her, taking grandmother's hand in hers. Father reasserted his demands but Sara was not paying attention, she was totally focused on the supine figure before her. Finally Sara gathered all her courage and drew herself up on the bed laying her head on grandmother's chest. Within the next moment grandmother opened her eyes, smiled warmly at the small figure resting peacefully on her chest. Speaking softly, as she stroked Sara's hair, grandmother spoke her final words. "It has been a wonderful life Sara, a wonderful and fulfilling life." With that she closed her eyes and reassumed her peaceful countenance. She died later that day.

Sara was blessed that day for she encountered, throughout her young life, the creative energy of a woman who lived a full and productive life. Sara could "see" with her own eyes the satisfied expression of her grandmother relinquishing her life easily to the unknown aware that she creatively lived without regret. Finally, Sara could "touch" the energy of her grandmother's creative essence, and "embrace" those important words that would be applied to Sara's life while, in the same instance, blessing her with a warm and loving memory of her grandmother. Within the blessing and message of this story, can we look at ourselves and say with confidence that we too have lived a wonderful and fulfilling life, that we have not retired with our music still in us? Learn to see, touch, and embrace your own potential for empowerment and may the creative force be with you.

Bibliography

Abbott, Bud, and Castello, Lou. *Who's On First*. Video. UAV Entertainment, Fort Mill, SC, 1

Ackerman, Diane. *Deep Play*. New York: Vintage Books, 1999

Bathum, Mike. *Portfolio of Illustrated 4-Step Art Projects*. New Jersey: Prentice-Hall, 1984

Benke, Britta. *O'Keeffe*. New York: Barnes and Noble Books, 2001

Blakeslee, Thomas. *The Right Brain: A New Understanding of the Unconscious Mind and Its Creative Powers*. New York: Berkley Books, 1980

Capps, Donald. *Jesus, A Psychological Biography*. St. Louis: Chalice Press, 2000

Clark, Arthur C. *2001: A Space Odyssey*. New York: Penguin Putnam Inc,. 2000

Cramer, Richard Ben. *Joe Dimaggio, The Hero's Life*. New York: Simon and Schuster, 2000

Dash, Mike. *Tulipomania*. New York: Three Rivers Press, 1999

Grudin, Robert. *The Grace of Great Things: Creativity and Innovation*. New York: Ticknor and Fields,1990

Hanh,Thich Nhat. *Plum Village Chanting and Recitation Book*. Berkeley: Parallax Press, 2000

Kirsch, Jonathan. *The Harlot by the Side of the Road*. New York: Ballantine Books,1997

Mandela, Nelson. *InauguralAddress*. South Africa,1994

May, Rollo. *The Cry For Myth*. New York: W.W. Norton, 1991

McNiff, Shaun. *Art As Medicine*. Boston: Shambhala Publications,1992

Metzer, Bruce M., and Murphy, Roland E., Editors. *The New Oxford Annotated Bible, The Revised StandardVersion*. New York: Oxford University Press, 1991

Missildine, W. Hugh, M.D. *Your Inner Child of the Past*. New York: Pocket Books, 1963

Palmer, Parker. *The Active Life; Wisdom for Work, Creativity, and Caring*. San Francisco: Harper 1990

Remen, Rachel Naomi, M.D. *Kitchen Table Wisdom*. New York: Riverhead Books, 1996

Richards, M.C. *Centering; In Pottery, Poetry, and the Person*. Middletown, Connecticut: Wesleyan University Press, 1964

Rubin, Theodore, M.D. *Compassion and Self-Hate*. New York: Touchstone, 1998

Rupp, Joyce. *FreshBread*. Notre Dame: Ave Maria Press, 1985

Sanford, John. *The Kingdom Within*. New York: HarperCollins, 1987

ISBN 1-41204594-0